THE MEDICAL MAN AND THE WITCH
DURING THE RENAISSANCE

PUBLICATIONS OF THE INSTITUTE OF THE HISTORY OF MEDICINE

THE JOHNS HOPKINS UNIVERSITY

THIRD SERIES   VOLUME II

THE MEDICAL MAN AND THE WITCH DURING THE RENAISSANCE

BY

GREGORY ZILBOORG, M. D.

THE HIDEYO NOGUCHI LECTURES

NEW YORK
COOPER SQUARE PUBLISHERS, INC.
1969

Originally Published 1935
Published by Cooper Square Publishers, Inc.
59 Fourth Avenue, New York, N. Y. 10003
Standard Book Number 8154-0314-3
Library of Congress Catalog Card No. 79-97605

Printed in the United States of America
NOBLE OFFSET PRINTERS, INC.
NEW YORK 3, N. Y.

TABLE OF CONTENTS

PREFACE

The history of psychiatry is undoubtedly one of the most fascinating subjects of medical history, and yet so far it has been badly neglected. This is hard to understand, as the psychiatrist has more affinity to the humanities than any medical man. His biographical approach to the patient is historical in character and as a matter of fact I have hardly ever met a psychiatrist who was not interested in the history of medicine.

The explanation for this neglect is probably to be sought in the extraordinary difficulty of the subject. Medical history cannot be understood without a careful consideration of the cultural backgrounds with all their implications. This is true of the history of all medical disciplines, but most especially of the history of psychiatry. It is relatively easy to understand a physician's ideas about mental diseases, and still easier to ascertain what his methods of treatment were. But it is extraordinarily difficult to understand the physician's object, the mentally sick man of former times.

Our psychological knowledge is the result of studies made on contemporaries. We are inclined to assume that the mental reactions of man were always the same. Many historical interpretations given by psychiatrists suffer through the fact that they were made on this assumption. St. Francis or Leonardo da Vinci have been analyzed as though they were our contemporaries.

The historian's procedure is different. He does not start on the hypothesis that he knows man. All that is known to him are man's creations as transmitted in documents, literary and otherwise. By examining them he endeavours to reconstruct a world that is gone and in this way to gain access to an individual mind. He will find man very different in different periods of history.

The task is infinitely more arduous still as soon as pathological phenomena are concerned. Mental reactions that would be decidedly morbid if they were met with in our society today, may have been perfectly normal in former societies. It is only through a very careful analysis of a period that we may come to a judgment.

The problem of witchcraft discussed in these three lectures is a very good illustration of the subject. No doubt many women who ended their lives at the stake were psychopathic personalities, not so the men who persecuted them. It was society as a whole that be-

lieved in witchcraft as a result of a definite philosophy. And the fact that a man arose who did not
share the common opinion, but opposed it, undoubtedly meant a turning-point, not only in the history of
psychiatry but in the history of human thought and
human behavior at large.

I greatly welcome the fact that so able a psychiatrist as Dr. Gregory Zilboorg has entered the historical field. A Russian by birth, he was trained in
sociology and medicine, became a student of Bekh-
terev and graduated from The Psycho-neurological
Institute in Petrograd. After having taken an active
part in the Russian revolution he came to this country
and worked for six years in Bloomingdale Hospital.
While studying psychoanalysis in Berlin he came to
see me in Leipzig and we have been in constant
touch ever since. An excellent linguist, like so many
Russians, with a broad cultural background, he is
best equipped for historical studies.

The present lectures are not an incidental study,
but the result of many years of research that will
finally lead to a History of Medical Psychology that
Dr. Zilboorg is preparing in coöperation with Dr.
G. W. Henry. Dr. Zilboorg recognized that witchcraft is the central problem in the development of

ix

occidental psychiatry. In the changing attitude towards witchcraft, modern psychiatry was born as a medical discipline. And Johann Weyer appears, not merely as the humanitarian as he is usually pictured, but as a physician of great clinical insight. The textbooks of medical history will have to be revised in this respect.

We are looking forward to Dr. Zilboorg's further studies in the field of psychiatric history.

HENRY E. SIGERIST

THE JOHNS HOPKINS UNIVERSITY
FEBRUARY, 1935

Witches producing hail

(After Ulrich Molitor's *Landis*)

LECTURE ONE

THE PHYSIOLOGICAL AND PSYCHOLOGICAL ASPECTS OF THE *MALLEUS MALEFICARUM* (*THE WITCH'S HAMMER*)

1

Ladies and Gentlemen:

St. Remy curing a man
possessed by the devil.

THE very subject matter of this lecture, the first of the series on " The Medical Man and the Witch during the Renaissance," is somewhat of a departure from a tradition which has been established for many years in the field of the history of medicine. Whether as a result of the natural propensity of man — even of the very scientific man — to turn towards "the brighter side" of things, or as a result of the scientist's tendency towards too great detachment, studies of the Renaissance of the Arts and Sciences have always been made in a psychological atmosphere of great scientific cheer. The student of the period, absorbed in the contemplation of the scientific ravages which the so-called dark ages perpetrated on the classical world, put himself in the place of the actual or imaginary truth-seeking and freedom-loving man of the time, and thus having identified himself with an actual or imaginary libertarian, he tended to overlook the other, as yet unpolished side of the medal, or at least to over-emphasize the bright side of the scientific and social awakening which was the Renaissance. Hence, it would seem that the proper perspective of the age to be considered in these lectures became somewhat distorted; scientific achievements were pushed into the foreground and the gruesome picture of witchcraft and witch-hunting was relegated to the background, either as an anachronistic survival of the receding past, or as a purely religious phenomenon based on ignorance only. It was charged up to the Church and its alleged maleficent influence, and thus quite obviously the real psycho-sociological meaning of the phenomenon in general, and particularly its rôle in the evolution of medical science, was not — as it could not be — fully appreciated. This is perhaps the reason why such a vital part of medicine as psychopathology, or as it is sometimes called, medical psychology, occupies even today a somewhat isolated and at times scientifically not too respectable, or not sufficiently respected, position in the system of medical sciences. For towards the close of the Middle

2

Ages science was forced away from human psychology, so that even the great endeavors of Erasmus and his friend Vives, as the best representatives of humanism, did not suffice to bring about a rapprochement, and psychopathology had to trail centuries behind the developmental trend of general medicine and surgery. As a matter of fact, and as will be shown in the second lecture, the divorcement of medical science from psychopathology was so definite that the latter was almost totally relegated to the domain of theology and ecclesiastic and civil law — two fields which naturally became further and further removed from medicine. The medical man of the Renaissance in order to study medicine had to learn Greek, improve his viciated Latin, and ponder over the texts of Hippocrates, Celsus, Alexander of Tralles, and particularly that of Galen; while to study psychopathology he would have had to steep himself in the obscure mysticism of St. Augustine, or of Michael Psellos' demonology (XIth century), or Nider's *Formicarius* (early XVth century), or Kraemer's and Sprenger's *Malleus Maleficarum*, or (about a century later) Jean Bodin's learned legalistic treatises. All these were authoritative statements of irrevocable and incontestable truths, as revealed

3

or as reasserted by the ecclesiastic and secular arms of the Law, and they allowed of no systematic skepticism nor even of simple doubt. How medicine met these difficulties will be shown in the later lectures. For the time being, it will suffice to say that medicine stood aloof for many decades, if not for centuries, and hence a singular picture reveals itself to the student of medical history: while anatomy and general pathology soon developed into a solid scientific structure, medical psychology was still but an amorphous, mysterious, and untouchable mass, even more obscure than human knowledge had become after the destruction of the Alexandrian library. To use the words of Binz, it was a time " in which science and art were reborn; but in those days, when people were painting and sculpting anew and once more turned towards investigation and writing, the making of new discoveries and new inventions, when the old classical world and bookprinting seemed to recast the face of western civilization — in those very days humanity stood in one respect on a lower level of mental development than do some of the primitive races of today." [1] To the ear of the self-conscious, civilized man, this statement might ring as grossly exag-

---

[1] Binz, Carl, *Doctor Johann Weyer* (Bonn, 1885), p. 3.

gerated. It is not untrue, however, and if one ponders over the nature of the obscure enormities of witchcraft, sorcery, demonolatry, tortures, hanging and burning, one feels convinced that a comparative ethnological study of primitive beliefs and customs would throw a great deal of light on the nature of this aspect of medical history as well as on the theology of that time. The importance of the theological documents themselves as the best source of clinical material cannot be overlooked. It is for this reason that, when one tries to gain an understanding not only of the pathological psychology of some aspects of human life during the Renaissance, but also of the clinical psychopathology as it was hidden, so to speak, from the medical man, one's attention naturally turns toward such documents as the *Malleus Maleficarum*.

2

The *Malleus Maleficarum* was conceived by two Dominican monks, Johann Sprenger and Heinrich Kraemer (Institoris), both Inquisitors appointed by Pope Innocent VIII to act in Northern Germany and some territories along the Rhine. Acting on the authority of the Pope, who on December 5th, 1484, issued a special Bull for the purpose (*Summis deside-*

rantes affectibus), these two Inquisitors set out to consolidate their position and to uncover, apprehend, and try witches and wizards. However, they were met with considerable resistance. Some of the clergy were apparently loath to co-operate with them — one bishop politely and firmly closed the door before Institoris (Kraemer) — and the population not infrequently came out to meet them with threats and clinched fists. In order to secure proper support on the part of ecclesiastic and secular authorities, the two friars composed the *Malleus Maleficarum* and took definite steps to make it authoritative and official. To achieve this end they asked the Dean of the University of Cologne to summon a meeting of the Faculty of Theology. On the nineteenth day of May, 1487, the professors of the above-named Faculty met, Dean Lambertus de Monte presiding. Sprenger and Kraemer appeared in person asking for the endorsement of their book. The Dean, who had apparently perused the manuscript beforehand, was the first to sign an endorsement adding to his signature some carefully worded explanatory remarks; four of the seven professors followed suit. This, however, seemed unsatisfactory to the Inquisitors. They then composed their own form of endorsement, pressing for

6

an immediate approbation. This time the remaining three professors had also apparently to affix their signatures, and the two Dominican brothers found themselves in full possession of a definite and official endorsement by the academic authorities — all the signatures having been duly certified by an official notary. This done, the two men produced the royal order issued from Brussels on November 6, 1486, specifically mentioning the Papal Bull, *Summis desiderantes affectibus*, and giving official support to the two Inquisitors in the discharge of their holy duty.[2] The King of Rome, Maximilian, thus gave the two Dominicans the full legal support of civil authority. With the document duly examined and the authenticity of the royal seal established, Kraemer solicited and obtained permission to prepare a number of certified copies of the letter of endorsement and approbation, these to serve as a document for official use whenever and wherever the two holy brothers would meet with difficulty.

These were the steps that launched the publication of the *Malleus* some time between 1487 and 1489 and the practical application of its thesis. This book, "A heavy volume in quarto, is so insane, so raw and

[2] Binz, Carl, *op. cit.*, p. 9.

cruel, and it leads to such terrible conclusions, that never before or since did such a unified combination of horrible characteristics flow from a human pen. Many feelings well up in the present-day reader who is forced to work through its text: feelings of oppression, disgust, mournful sadness, and national shame. It is difficult to say which of these happen to predominate at any one time." [3] The volume became the leading, if not the only, textbook of the Inquisition, and before 1669 it was printed ten times and in less than another century it went through nine more editions. It was not translated into any modern language until the twentieth century; a German edition appeared in 1906 and an English one in 1928. [4]

The thesis of the *Malleus* is as simple as it seems to us horrible. It is divided into three parts. The first part represents an argument which attempts to prove the existence of witchcraft and witches, or to be more correct, to prove by argumentation rather than by factual demonstration that he who does not believe in the existence of witches is either in honest error or polluted with heresy. The second part is devoted to

[3] *Ibid.*, p. 10.
[4] *Der Hexenhammer*, translated by J. W. R. Schmidt; *Malleus Maleficarum*, translated by Rev. Montague Summers.

what we would call today clinical reports. It tells of various types of witches and of the different methods one should use to identify a witch. To use modern terminology, it describes the clinical pictures and the various ways of arriving at a diagnosis. The third part deals with the legal forms of examining and sentencing a witch. It goes into the details of legal technicalities and the technique of delivering a witch from the devil or to the secular arm of justice for execution, in most cases by burning. It is not a dispassionate, cold, legalistic treatise; it is, rather, polemical, argumentative, scornful or threatening in tone, and uncompromising. It is written with firm conviction and a fervent zeal which made the authors totally anesthetic to the sight of wounds and blood, or to the smell of burning human flesh. However, the sadistic details which are so shocking to the man of today, do not concern us here. A consideration of these would add nothing to our knowledge of human propensities and would, moreover, tend considerably to obscure the calm judgment of the facts under consideration. It is this element of emotional bias that is probably responsible for the mistaken view that the *Malleus Maleficarum* was in a large measure responsible for many of the cruelties

9

of witch-hunting perpetrated all over Europe for a period of almost three hundred years, and that Innocent VIII, by his specific mention of the horrors of witchcraft and of the two zealous Dominican monks in the *Summis desiderantes affectibus*, initiated the terrors of the Inquisition. As a matter of historical fact, witches and their craft had been treated with suspicion and cruelty since time immemorial, even long before monotheism was established. Official prosecution of witches by the Church has its own history, which began long before and continued long after Pope Innocent VIII occupied the throne of St. Peter. While a detailed history of this problem is unnecessary in considering our present subject, a better perspective will be gained if, before examining certain specific features of the *Malleus*, we point out a few of the highlights in the development of witchcraft and the Inquisition.

3

It is hardly necessary to dwell on the fact that from the most primitive beginnings of human history, man believed in the existence of spirits and magic, and that from the earliest days of his existence on earth, he began to ascribe various unusual

10

phenomena of nature to the activities of evil spirits. This naturally led him to believe that any pathology in human behavior must be due to an evil spirit — hence the theory of demoniacal possessions must be as old as man is old. For example, the Egyptian stele, kept in the Bibliothèque Nationale in Paris, relates the story of what we would call a demoniacal possession with which a young princess of the twentieth dynasty of Pharaohs was afflicted until the Egyptian God Khons finally cured her. In other words, even thirteen centuries before the Christian Era some connection was felt between being possessed by the devil and the need for being cured. However, these psychopathological manifestations, while always skirting the confines of medicine, never established a successful contact with medicine until three thousand years after the Egyptian princess was cured by Khons. The brief interlude of active psychiatric study which marks the period between the time Hippocrates wrote *On the Sacred Disease* and the death of Galen, i. e., a period of approximately seven hundred years, was frequently interrupted by open persecution of many mentally sick who were mistaken for witches, magicians, or necromancers. Under Emperors Augustus, Tiberius, and Septimius Severus, these used to be

11

exiled. The populace among the Celts, the Franks, and undoubtedly other peoples, frequently took the law into their own hands and killed witches. Then, too, it should not be forgotten that the Old Testament, as well as the New, deals frequently with the problem of casting out devils, enjoining believers to exterminate the witches and wizards. Despite the fact that in the third century of the Christian Era the witch was not as yet clearly differentiated from those possessed by good angels, and that some of the Fathers of the Church dealt with them kindly (Tertullian), the negative attitude towards possessions began to be clearly crystallized in the fourth century under Emperor Constantine. From St. Augustine's time forward, the struggle against the devil became one of the most active and most persistent preoccupations of both churchman and layman. The maleficent power of such things as the witch's knot, or the witch's ladder, was recognized and feared all over Europe, as it was supposed to bring evil into one's home and control the elements of nature to the extent of raising storms at sea and causing shipwrecks. This "witch's ladder" was feared as much in Scotland as it was in Italy (*la ghirlanda delle streghe*). It was this fear of the unknown and the incomprehensible that invaded the minds of law-givers as much as those of the populace, so that the *Codex Theodosianus* was not any more clement about magic or witchcraft than was the very strict ancient Frankish law codified and known as *Lex Salica*. By the ninth century of our era ecclesiastic and secular tradition, instead of eradicating, found itself fully accepting the perennial tradition, and the Council of Paris (829) admonished the secular courts to concur in the sentences pronounced by the Bishops. According to Summers,[5] from that time on the penalty for sorcery was death, although as early as the very beginning of the seventh century Pope Gregory I (590-604) was aroused to official action against sorcerers and masters in black magic.

The differentiation between a mentally sick person, a witch, and a heretic became less and less definite, so that towards the middle of the thirteenth century these became synonymous in the mind of man. To-wards the middle of the fifteenth century this differentiation was scarcely ever made, nor were such distinctions even possible — for reasons which will be apparent later when we deal directly with the

[5] Summers, Rev. Montague. Cf. his Introduction to the English translation of the *Malleus Maleficarum*.

13

evidence cited by the *Malleus*. It is interesting to note in this connection that the first Papal Bull dealing directly with witchcraft was that of Gregory IX in 1233, and that the first extremely strict laws against heretics promulgated by lay authority were those of Frederick II, the colorful contemporary of Pope Gregory IX. These facts may be of more than passing interest, and their significance, if properly understood, would perhaps provide us with a possible clue to what happened two hundred and fifty years later at the height of the Renaissance. Frederick II did not enjoy the reputation of a great believer and at his court many a free-thinker found cordial hospitality; he was even suspected of himself harboring heretical ideas since he made friends with some of the prominent Arabian scholars of his day. It was Frederick II who is supposed to have uttered the apostatic statement that the world's greatest impostors were Moses, Jesus, and Mohammed. Yet it was Frederick II who was one of the very first to banish, punish, and confiscate the property of heretics. While these measures might have been dictated by political expediency and egocentric motives of an economic nature, it is difficult to see in these facts merely a fortuitous play of circumstance. We might

14

recall that Frederick's " free-thinking " was not an isolated phenomenon, and that the thirteenth century presented the first awakening from the medieval sleep that followed the downfall of Rome. It was a sort of pre-Renaissance of the Arts and Sciences: in medicine, Arnald of Villanova, Mundinus, and Albertus Magnus; in theology, Thomas Aquinas; in philosophy and sciences, John Scotus, Alexander of Hales, and Roger Bacon — all marked a definite departure from established tradition. Mundinus, an historical forerunner of Vesalius, dared to look again into the human body instead of into traditional writings to learn anatomy, and both Scotus and Alexander of Hales definitely expressed doubt as to the devil's power to produce mental disease.

It was apparently this first awakening of scientific skepticism that aroused the authorities, lay and ecclesiastic, to a measure of self-defense, thus sounding the first signal of persecution. The very busy centuries that followed, with the conquest of new territories and the subjugation of the Mohammedan world, brought to a temporary halt both the natural growth of the spirit of doubt and the need for active persecution, but both reappeared and reasserted themselves towards the close of the fifteenth century. The question then arises, what was the actual attitude of the world towards the problem of witchcraft? That there was opposition towards the traditional views, is evidenced by the polemical tone of many a page of the *Malleus*. But this opposition was not yet sufficiently crystallized; moreover, even if it were, we must not forget that when the *Malleus* was first published hardly three decades had elapsed since books began to be printed, and therefore no real published opposition was possible. The vernacular protests of Montaigne and Rabelais were unthinkable at that time. Hence one could not expect any great popularization of scientific opposition to the universal "endemic persecutory mania"[6] in the throes of which the world lived at the time. What the nature of this "persecutory mania" was, or rather, what the psychological factors were which created an atmosphere conducive to such a "mass psychosis," such a "folie à foule," as it were, will be answered at least in part when Sprenger and Kraemer tell us what they considered was the witch's chief sin. In the meantime, let us seek the views of those who felt impelled to authorize the persecution of witches.

[6] Binz, Carl. *op. cit.*

16

4

The Bull of Innocent VIII referred to above reads as follows:

"Desiring with the most heartfelt anxiety, even as Our Apostleship requires, that the Catholic Faith should especially in this Our day increase and flourish everywhere, and that all heretical depravity should be driven far from the frontiers and bournes of the Faithful, We very gladly proclaim and even restate those particular means and methods whereby Our pious desire may obtain its wished effect, since when all errors are uprooted by Our diligent avocation as by the hoe of a provident husbandman, a zeal for, and the regular observance of, Our holy Faith will be all the more strongly impressed upon the hearts of the faithful.

"It has indeed lately come to Our ears, not without afflicting Us with bitter sorrow, that in some parts of Northern Germany, as well as in the provinces, townships, territories, districts, and dioceses of Mainz, Cologne, Trèves, Salzburg, and Bremen, many persons of both sexes, unmindful of their own salvation and straying from the Catholic Faith, have abandoned themselves to devils, incubi and succubi, and by their incantations, spells, conjurations, and other accursed charms and crafts, enormities and horrid offences, have slain infants yet in the mother's womb, as also the offspring of cattle, have blasted the produce of the earth, the grapes of the vine, the fruits of trees, nay, men and women, beasts of burthen, herd-beasts, as well as animals of other kinds, vineyards, orchards, meadows, pasture-land, corn, wheat, and all other cereals; these wretches furthermore afflict and torment men and women, beasts of burthen, herd-beasts, as well as animals of other kinds, with terrible and piteous pains and sore diseases, both internal and external; they hinder men from performing the sexual act and women from conceiving, whence husbands cannot know their wives nor wives receive their husbands; over and above this, they blasphemously renounce that Faith which is theirs by the Sacrament of Baptism, and at the instigation of the Enemy of Mankind they do not shrink from committing and perpetrating the foulest abominations and filthiest excesses to the deadly peril of their own souls, whereby they outrage the Divine Majesty and are a cause of scandal and danger to very many. And although Our dear sons Henry Kraemer and James Sprenger, Professors of

Theology, of the Order of Friars Preachers, have been by Letters Apostolic delegated as Inquisitors of these heretical pravities, and still are Inquisitors, the first in the aforesaid parts of Northern Germany, wherein are included those aforesaid townships, districts, dioceses, and other specified localities, and the second in certain territories which lie along the borders of the Rhine, nevertheless not a few clerics and lay folk of those countries, seeking too curiously to know more than concerns them, since in the aforesaid delegatory letters there is no express and specific mention by name of these provinces, townships, dioceses, and districts, and further since the two delegates themselves and the abominations they are to encounter are not designated in detailed and particular fashion, these persons are not ashamed to contend with the most unblushing effrontery that these enormities are not practised in those provinces, and consequently the aforesaid Inquisitors have no legal right to exercise their powers of inquisition in the provinces, townships, dioceses, districts, and territories, which have been rehearsed, and that the Inquisitors may not proceed to punish, imprison, and penalize criminals convicted of the heinous offences and many wickednesses which have been set forth.

Accordingly in the aforesaid provinces, townships, dioceses, and districts, the abominations and enormities in question remain unpunished not without open danger to the souls of many and peril of eternal damnation.

"Wherefore We, as is Our duty, being wholly desirous of removing all hindrances and obstacles by which the good work of the Inquisitors may be let and tarded, as also of applying potent remedies to prevent the disease of heresy and other turpitudes diffusing their poison to the destruction of many innocent souls, since Our zeal for the Faith especially incites us, lest that the provinces, townships, dioceses, districts, and territories of Germany, which We have specified, be deprived of the benefits of the Holy Office thereto assigned, by the tenor of these presents in virtue of Our Apostolic authority We decree and enjoin that the aforesaid Inquisitors be empowered to proceed to the just correction, imprisonment, and punishment of any persons, without let or hindrance, in every way as if the provinces, townships, dioceses, districts, territories, yea, even the persons and their crimes in this kind were named and particularly designated in Our letters. Moreover, for greater surety We extend these letters deputing this

authority to cover all the aforesaid provinces, townships, dioceses, districts, and territories, persons, and
crimes newly rehearsed, and We grant permission to
the aforesaid Inquisitors, to one separately or to
both, as also to Our dear son John Gremper, priest
of the diocese of Constance, Master of Arts, their
notary, or to any other public notary, who shall be
by them, or by one of them, temporarily delegated
to those provinces, townships, dioceses, districts, and
aforesaid territories, to proceed, according to the
regulations of the Inquisition, against any persons of
whatsoever rank and high estate, correcting, mulct-
ing, imprisoning, punishing, as their crimes merit,
those whom they have found guilty, the penalty
being adapted to the offence. Moreover, they shall
enjoy a full and perfect faculty of expounding and
preaching the word of God to the faithful, so often
as opportunity may offer and it may seem good to
them, in each and every parish church of the said
provinces, and they shall freely and lawfully perform
any rites or execute any business which may appear
advisable in the aforesaid cases. By Our supreme
authority We grant them anew full and complete
faculties.

" At the same time by Letters Apostolic We re-

quire Our venerable Brother, the Bishop of Strasburg, that he himself shall announce, or by some
other or others cause to be announced, the burthen
of Our Bull, which he shall solemnly publish when
and so often as he deems it necessary, or when he
shall be requested so to do by the Inquisitors or by
one of them. Nor shall he suffer them in disobedi-
ence to the tenor of these presents to be molested
or hindered by any authority whatsoever, but he shall
threaten all who endeavour to hinder or harass the
Inquisitors, all who oppose them, all rebels, of whatsoever rank, estate, position, pre-eminence, dignity,
or any condition they may be, or whatsoever privilege
of exemption they may claim, with excommunication,
suspension, interdict, and yet more terrible penalties,
censures, and punishment, as may seem good to him,
and that without any right of appeal, and if he will
he may by Our authority aggravate and renew these
penalties as often as he list, calling in, if so please
him, the help of the secular arm. . . ." [7]

From the above it is clear that towards the close
of the fifteenth century the concept of the witch expanded to immense proportions. She became the

[7] Summers, Rev. Montague, Introduction to his English translation of the *Malleus Maleficarum*, pp. xliii-xlv.

heretical enemy not only of the political and religious status of the age, but of nature itself. Pope Innocent VIII was criticized by many non-Catholic writers for this official expression of a pernicious belief in witches. Attempts were made to discredit him as a personality, because of his rather alluring past as a young and attractive Genoese layman. Needless to say, the Bull of Pope Innocent VIII had little to do with the young Genoese Giovanni Battista Cibo, and his *Summis desiderantes affectibus* is not a personal but an historical document of perfect historical continuity. Therefore one finds one's self in total agreement with Binz, who states: "What that loose Genoese Innocent VIII had raised to the rank of an ecclesiastic principle was reaffirmed at a somewhat later date with the same vehemence by the pious, good-natured and puritanical Adrian VI, the scholarly, high-standing teacher of Erasmus and the tutor of Karl V, the last Teuton to sit on the papal throne. In his decree of July 20, 1522, to the Inquisitor of Cremona," he stated almost literally the same things about witchcraft and witch-hunting as his predecessors and contemporaries of less exalted position.

The great scholar Johannes Trithemius, the younger contemporary of Friars Sprenger and Kraemer, a very learned and very kind man, did not depart from the same views. This Benedictine abbot "was a man whose friendship was sought by all important princes and scholars of his day. He was a man of whom a contemporary states that a goodness that could not be expressed in words rested upon his sturdy manly brow and that his pure and luminous eyes appeared to reflect a celestial light." It was this great personality who, at the request of Joachim of Brandeburg, whose guest he was at the time, composed a book called *Antipalus Maleficarum* in which, among other things dealing with the same subject, we read· "There is no part in our body that they (the witches) would not injure. Most of the time they make the human being possessed and thus they are left to the devils to be tortured with unheard of pains. They even get into carnal relations with them. . . . Unfortunately, the number of such witches is very great in every province; more than that, there is no locality too small for a witch to find. Yet Inquisitors and Judges who could avenge these open offenses against God and Nature are so few and far between. Man and beast die as a result of the evil of these women and no one thinks of the fact that these things are perpetrated by witches.

Many suffer constantly of severest diseases and are not even aware that they are bewitched." [8]

We thus have here an authoritative statement of great and rather pernicious significance to medicine, more particularly to psychological medicine, since no method of differentiation between bodily suffering caused by a legitimate pathogenic agent and that caused by a witch or the devil is given, and since what was done by a witch should not be treated medically, but dealt with legally. The whole field of medicine is thereby excluded from everything that might be ascribed to the devil or his witches. The disease which we would call today organic (in those days it was called *natural*) became a rather small entity still left in the hands of a physician, while the disease which we would call today neurotic, functional, or psychogenic (in those days it was called *supernatural*) was definitely decreed to be and to remain in the hands of the law. The number of these diseases was increasing very rapidly: the number of individuals afflicted soon reached the mark of many hundreds of thousands and the clinical entities embraced every conceivable physiological function and every conceivable anatomical structure. However,

[8] Binz, Carl, *op. cit.*, p. 7.

we might note in passing that, as was partly alluded to in the Bull of Innocent VIII, the majority of symptoms in so far as they were connected with physiological reactions were related to sexual and gastro-intestinal functions — the two great domains of modern neuroses. Thus there appears to be little doubt that, even on the basis of the few illustrative statements cited above, we are justified in saying that the world, particularly the official world, was in a state of constant panic, and that those who thought they had good reason to be afraid hopelessly confused human illness with sedition.

No one summarized this state of affairs better than our contemporary, the Reverend Montague Summers, who today, like many of his predecessors in the fifteenth and sixteenth centuries, combines great and profound learning with no less great and no less profound belief in the existence of witches. He thus states of Henry VIII: " When, as so speedily happened, he wearied of Anne Boleyn, he openly gave it as his opinion that he had ' made this marriage seduced by witchcraft; and that this was evident because God did not permit them to have any male issue.' " Again: " That there were witches in England is very certain," and again: he cites the case of a man tried by the Court of Urban VIII because he caused " a statue of wax to be made of Urban VIII in order that its dissolution might insure that of the Pope." Thus, credence is given to the view that witches will cause sterility as well as regicide. Physiology having become so obscurely and so intimately knit together with politics and dogma, and in a manner which at times leaves the individual totally unaware of the cause of his trouble (Trithemius), one can easily see how a logical conclusion suggested itself which again is best expressed in the words of our contemporary Reverend Summers: " Their objects may be summed up as the abolition of monarchy, the abolition of private property and of inheritance, the abolition of marriage, the abolition of order, the total abolition of all religion. It was against this that the Inquisition had to fight, and who can be surprised if, when faced with so vast a conspiracy, the methods employed by the Holy Office may not seem — if the terrible conditions are conveniently forgotten — a little drastic, a little severe? There can be no doubt that had this most excellent tribunal continued to enjoy its full prerogative and the full exercise of its salutary powers, the world at large would be in a far happier and far more orderly position to-day. Historians may point out diversities and dissimilarities between the teaching of the Waldenses, the Albigenses, the Henricians, the Poor Men of Lyons, the Cathari, the Vaudois, the Bogomiles, and Manichees, but they were in reality branches and variants of the same dark fraternity, just as the Third International, the Anarchists, the Nihilists, and the Bolsheviks are in every sense, save the mere label, entirely identical." [9]

This is the mood in which Reverend Montague Summers translates the *Malleus Maleficarum*, and it is the mood in which it was written by the two Dominican friars four hundred and fifty years previously.

5

The dividing line between physical or mental illness and heresy or apostasy having been all but effaced, the physiology and the psychology of the day had to be adjusted accordingly. No man, woman, or child could escape the new field of demoniacal pathology. " So in the prosecutions at Würzburg we find that there were condemned boys of ten and eleven, two choir boys aged twelve, ' a boy of twelve years old in one of the lower forms of school,' ' the

[9] Summers, Rev. Montague, *op. cit.*, p. xviii.

two young sons of the Prince's cook, the eldest fourteen, the younger twelve years old,' several pages
and seminarists, as well as a number of young girls
amongst whom ' a child of nine or ten years old and
her little sister were involved.' " [10] As to the objections which were apparently raised that we might
be dealing with delusions on the part of the alleged witches, these are repeatedly disposed of in
the following manner: " Therefore those err who
say that there is no such thing as witchcraft, but that
it is purely imaginary, even although they do not
believe that devils exist except in the imagination of
the ignorant and vulgar, and the natural accidents
which happen to a man he wrongly attributes to some
supposed devil. For the imagination of some men is
so vivid that they think they see actual figures and
appearances which are but the reflection of their
thoughts, and then these are believed to be the
apparitions of evil spirits or even the spectres of
witches. But this is contrary to the true faith, which
teaches us that certain angels fell from heaven and
are now devils, and we are bound to acknowledge
that by their very nature they can do many wonderful
things which we cannot do. And those who try to

[10] Summers, Rev. Montague, *op. cit.*, p. xix.

induce others to perform such evil wonders are called witches. And because infidelity in a person who has been baptized is technically called heresy, therefore such persons are plainly heretics." [11] However, even the authors of the *Malleus* stand ready to admit that on occasion the statement of a witch might be an expression of a delusion rather than of a fact; although they are firm believers in transvection, that is, in the capacity of a witch to transport herself or to be transported bodily through the air, they admit that at times this transvection is but a figure of the imagination; yet, this does not shake their belief that the pathogenic agent remains the same, i. e., the devil: ". . . although those women imagine they are riding with the devil, who calls himself by some such name and throws a glamor before their eyes. And the third point is this, that the act of riding abroad may be merely illusory, since the devil has extraordinary power over the minds of those who have given themselves up to him, so that what they do in pure imagination, they believe they have actually and really done in the body." It is clear that even if a delusion is taken as such, the cause was considered impure, the fact of

[11] *Malleus Maleficarum* (English edition), pp. 2-3.

the delusion a sin, and the mental illness a criminal act performed by the ill will of the patient. Such an attitude would naturally raise the accusation of ignorance and the two Inquisitors might have been suspected of discarding completely what little there was of scientific physiology which, albeit in viciated form, still bore the authoritative names of Aristotle, Galen, and their Arabian messengers like Avicenna; the authors of the *Malleus* repeatedly hasten to add that theirs is the task of refuting the unbeliever, but not that of discarding the authorities of the past, for least of all would they ever discard any authority, lay or ecclesiastic, pagan or Christian, unless it be the authority of the devil and his servants. Hence they state: ". . . devils by their art do bring about evil effects through witchcraft, yet it is true that without the assistance of some agent (as we would say today: without an exogenous factor. — G. Z.) they cannot make any form, either substantial or accidental, and we do not maintain that they can inflict damage without the assistance of some agent, but with such an agent diseases, and any other human passions and ailments, can be brought about and these are real and true." [12] Hence, these "bodily ills and ailments

[12] *Ibid.*, p. 11.

31

are certainly not invisible, nay rather they are evident to the senses, therefore they can be brought about by devils."

Yet, while referring to St. Augustine and "many credible witnesses that it would seem impudent to deny it," the question of differential diagnosis inevitably imposed itself upon the mind of man. How was one to differentiate under these circumstances a natural affliction from a supernatural one which showed the same symptoms and signs? To answer this question the authors of the *Malleus* try to leave no doubt as to their respect for traditional medicine. Quoting St. Augustine, they say: "Wherefore St. Augustine (*de civitate Dei* V) where he resolves a certain question of two brothers who fell ill and were cured simultaneously, approves the reasoning of Hippocrates rather than that of an Astronomer. For Hippocrates answered that it was owing to the identity of their horoscopes. For the Physician's answer was better, since he adduced the more powerful and immediate cause." [13] And further: "Nevertheless it sometimes happens that the devil is permitted to inflict only so small a vexation on a man that, through some strong contrary disposition, it

[13] *Ibid.*, p. 33.

may be totally removed; and then some herbs or harmonies can so dispose of man's body to the contrary that the vexation is totally removed. For example, the devil may at times vex a man with the affliction of sadness; but so weakly that herbs and harmonies which are capable of causing a swelling and uplifting of the spirits, which are contrary emotions to sadness, can totally remove sadness." [14]

Thus the *Malleus*, not being unmindful of medical therapeutic measures, makes more than one concession to medicine. It even admits that a more serious affliction than a slight vexation with sadness might prove to be amenable to scientific rather than criminological treatment. "Of the same opinion are Blessed Albert, in his commentary on *S. Luke* ix, and Nicolas of Lyra and Paul of Burgos, on I. *Samuel* xvi. The last-named homilist comes to this conclusion: that it must be allowed that those possessed by a devil can not only be relieved, but even entirely delivered by means of material things, understanding that in the latter case they are not very fiercely molested. And he proves this by reasoning as follows: Devils cannot alter corporeal matter just at their will, but only by bringing together complemen-

[14] *Ibid.*, p. 41.

33

tary active and passive agents, as Nicolas says. In the same way some material object can cause in the human body a disposition which makes it susceptible to the operations of the devil. For example, according to physicians, mania very much predisposes a man to dementia, and consequently to demoniac obsession: therefore if, in such a case, the predisposing passive agent be removed, it will follow that the active affliction of the devil will be cured." [15] While the authors of the *Malleus* are inclined to agree cautiously with the above view, and attempt to make a bow, as it were, to medical science, they do so not originally but by citing (with reservation, of course) their more liberal predecessors or contemporaries. They never fail, even while agreeing, to raise the all-important question as to whether the use of such material methods, though they may be effective, is at all lawful. We shall have the opportunity to return to this question later. In the meantime, it is fair to say that the *Malleus* is definitely diffident about "natural" methods of therapy, for it states as a conviction that "no witchcraft can be removed by any natural power, although it can be assuaged." [16] True, the authors were aware

[15] *Ibid.*, p. 178.   [16] *Ibid.*, p. 161.

34

that natural, non-magic power, such as music, had
been used for ages in the treatment of the mentally
sick—the authority of the Bible, relating to the
effect of music on the demented Saul, could hardly
be conveniently refuted by such pious men. Hence
the explicit statement: " And as for that concerning
I, *Kings* xvi: that Saul, who was vexed by a devil,
was alleviated when David played his harp before
him, and that the devil departed, etc. It must be
known that it is quite true that by the playing of the
harp, and the natural virtue of that harmony, the
affliction of Saul was to some extent relieved, inas-
much as that music did somewhat calm his senses
through hearing; through which calming he was
made less prone to that vexation. But the reason
why the evil spirit departed when David played the
harp was because of the might of the Cross, which
is clearly enough shown by the gloss, where it says:
David was learned in music, skilful in the different
notes and harmonious modulations. He shows the
essential unity by playing each day in various modes.
David repressed the evil spirit by the harp, not because there was so much virtue in the harp, but it was
made in the sign of a cross, being a cross of wood
with the strings stretched across. And even at that

time the devils fled from this." [17] It is quite clear that the *Malleus*, placing as it does a powerful therapeutic Cross in the hands of the King of ancient Israel a thousand years before the advent of Christ, relegates to the devil the whole field of pathology " For it is the practice of Scripture and of speech to name every unclean spirit Diabolus, from Dia, that is Two, and Bolus, that is Morsel; for he kills two things, the body and the soul. And this is in accordance with etymology, although in Greek *Diabolus* means shut in Prison, which also is apt, since he is not permitted to do as much harm as he wishes." [18] This passage, despite its laughable infantile philology, is of great significance because it demonstrates an unbending and implacable state of mind regardless of fact. The *Malleus*, having set out to prove and not to test a point, is bound to mobilize and set into action any argument available. The point to prove was that only good comes from God and all evil comes from the devil, although always with God's permission. It is interesting, in this respect, to note how zealously and jealousy the *Malleus* musters up every possible authority and argument to warn against ascribing even by innuendo anything more, or any-

[17] *Ibid.*, p. 41.   [18] *Ibid.*, p. 30.

thing less, to the devil than evil; it recalls St. Augustine (*de civitate Dei* V), citing: "If anyone attributes human affairs to Fate, meaning by Fate the Will and the Power of God, let him keep his opinion but amend his tongue."

This being the case, what was the domain of pathology, so carefully and persistently supervised or managed by the devil? The *Malleus,* as has been shown, makes some concessions to medicine and to physicians, but it goes on to say that aside from the multifarious ways in which the devils may produce various calamities, "they have six ways of injuring humanity. And one is, to induce an evil love in a man for a woman, or in a woman for a man. The second is to plant hatred or jealousy in anyone. The third is to bewitch them so that a man cannot perform the genital act with a woman, or conversely a woman with a man; or by various means to procure an abortion, as has been said before. The fourth is to cause some disease in any of the human organs. The fifth, to take away life. The sixth, to deprive them of reason." [19] Points three, four and six obviously embrace the greatest part, if not the whole field, of medicine. True, here

[19] *Ibid.,* p. 115.

and there one finds reference to various sociological causes of mental disease — the sudden loss of property or money for instance — as well as to such frankly "natural" diseases as epilepsy and leprosy, and even to such conditions as sleep-walking, but the *Malleus* finds it impossible entirely to absolve the devil even in these conditions. Thus: "Devils, by means of witches, so afflict their innocent neighbours with temporal losses, that they are as it were compelled, first to beg the suffrages of witches, and at length to submit themselves to their counsels; as many experiences have taught us." [20] As to sleep-walking, "Many think, and not without reason, that this is devils' work. For devils are of many different kinds, and some, who fell from the lower choir of Angels, are tortured as if for smaller sins with lighter punishments as well as the punishment of damnation which they must suffer eternally. And these cannot hurt anybody, at least not seriously, but for the most part carry out only practical jokes. And others are Incubi or Succubi, who punish men in the night, defiling them in the sin of lechery. It is not wonderful if they are given also to horse-play such as this." [21] And also in another place: "It is said of those who walk

[20] *Ibid.*, p. 96.   [21] *Ibid.*, pp. 105-106.

38

in their sleep during the night over high buildings without any harm, that it is the work of evil spirits who thus lead them; and many affirm that when such people are re-baptized they are much benefited. And it is wonderful that, when they are called by their own names, they suddenly fall to the earth, as if that name had not been given to them in proper form at their baptism." [22] As to epilepsy, " we have often found that certain people have been visited with epilepsy or the falling sickness by means of eggs which have been buried with dead bodies, especially the dead bodies of witches, together with other ceremonies of which we cannot speak, particularly when these eggs have been given to a person either in food or drink." [23] And, ". . . although greater difficulty may be felt in believing that witches are able to cause leprosy or epilepsy, since these diseases generally arise from some long-standing physical predisposition or defect, none the less it has some-times been found that even these have been caused by witchcraft. For in the diocese of Basel, in the district of Alsace and Lorraine, a certain honest labourer spoke roughly to a certain quarrelsome woman, and she angrily threatened him that she

[22] *Ibid.*, p. 186.   [23] *Ibid.*, p. 137.

would soon avenge herself on him. He took little notice of her; but on the same night he felt a pustule grow upon his neck, and he rubbed it a little, and found his whole face and neck puffed up and swollen, and a horrible form of leprosy appeared all over his body. He immediately went to his friends for advice, and told them of the woman's threat, and said that he would stake his life on the suspicion that this had been done to him by the magic art of that same witch. In short, the woman was taken, questioned, and confessed her crime. But when the judge asked her particularly about the reason for it, and how she had done it, she answered: 'When that man used abusive words to me, I was angry and went home; and my familiar began to ask the reason for my ill humor. I told him, and begged him to avenge me on the man. And he asked what I wanted him to do to him; and I answered that I wished he would always have a swollen face. And the devil went away and afflicted the man even beyond my asking; for I had not hoped that he would infect him with such sore leprosy.' And so the woman was burned." [24]
" And lastly, in the same diocese, in the territory of the Black Forest, a witch was being lifted by a goaler

[24] *Ibid.*, pp. 136-137.

on to the pile of wood prepared for her burning, and said: 'I will pay you'; and blew into his face. And he was at once afflicted with a horrible leprosy all over his body, and did not survive many days. For the sake of brevity, the fearful crimes of this witch, and many more instances which could be recounted, are omitted." [25]

These episodes, and the manner in which they are told, are characteristic of the *Malleus*: they are naïve, terse, credulous, and to the point, and are inspired with a spirit of hatred for women (witches). Of wizards the *Malleus* speaks but briefly, for its misogyny is as typical as it is pitiless and uncontrollable. Consequently, while it admits that the devil can do many things directly, it believes that he could not perform even one-hundredth of the things he does without the agency of witches. "For some learned men propound this reason; that there are three things in nature, the Tongue, an Ecclesiastic, and a Woman, which know no moderation in goodness or vice; and when they exceed the bounds of their condition they reach the greatest heights and the lowest depths of goodness and vice. When they are governed by a good spirit, they are

[25] *Ibid.*, p. 137.

most excellent in virtue; but when they are governed by an evil spirit, they indulge the worst possible vices." [26] "What else is woman but a foe to friendship, an unescapable punishment, a necessary evil, a natural temptation, a desirable calamity, a domestic danger, a delectable detriment, an evil of nature, painted with fair colours! Therefore if it be a sin to divorce her when she ought to be kept, it is indeed a necessary torture; for either we commit adultery by divorcing her, or we must endure daily strife." [27] Thus women, inferior by nature, lying, vicious, and hopelessly impure, are naturally the most serviceable and most willing tool of the devil. The *Malleus* supports its misogynous contentions by way of another characteristic excursion into infantile philology — the alleged derivation of the word *femina*; the word is supposed to come from *fe* and *minus*, the latter designating a defect in nature. Woman is also proven to be constitutionally inferior, because ". . . it should be noted that there was a defect in the formation of the first woman, since she was formed from a bent rib, that is, a rib of the breast, which is bent as it were in a contrary direction to a man. And

[26] *Ibid.*, p. 42.   [27] *Ibid.*, p. 43.

42

since through this defect she is an imperfect animal, she always deceives." [28]

Once having turned over the whole field of physical and mental pathology to the devil and his witches, the *Malleus* is particularly emphatic about mental pathology, " For if the secret wishes of a man are read in his face, and physicians can tell the thought of the heart from the heartbeats and the state of the pulse, all the more can such things be known by devils." [29] While the illustrative material is rather copious, it is all similar in nature to that of the case of the deluded witch who caused the poor laborer to be afflicted with leprosy. Quite naturally, the authors of the *Malleus* steadfastly stress faith and the typical formalistic logic of the time rather than facts and experience, for " it is better to prove . . . by the Scriptures, rather than by recent examples, since new things are always strengthened by old examples." [30] However, the *Malleus* does not limit itself to quoting the Scriptures. When it is necessary to prove that witches and wizards can turn into beasts and indulge in cannibalism, the reader is reminded that Circe changed the companions of Ulysses into beasts and

[28] *Ibid.*, p. 44.   [29] *Ibid.*, p. 111.   [30] *Ibid.*, p. 129.

that the companions of Diomedes were changed into birds.

After outlining their convictions and assigning to the Inquisition the business of ridding the world of devilish heresy, Sprenger and Kraemer apparently felt that in order to meet most effectively the demands of their arduous task, and particularly the possible skepticism of the clergy and of the monks for whose benefit the first two parts of the *Malleus* were written, a special physiological psychology had to be prepared, and some differential diagnostic criteria given. This they proceeded to do in their usual thoroughgoing manner.

6

Again and again the *Malleus* reminds the reader that no one can be a witch without entering a pact with the devil, and that all the heresies of witchcraft are a result of free choice on the part of the woman, for the doctrine of free will could not be alienated. "The sin of man proceeds from free-will, but the devil cannot destroy free-will, for this would militate against liberty; therefore the devil cannot be the cause of that or any other sin." Yet, the *Malleus* is fully aware that "sometimes the use of reason is entirely chained up; and this may be exemplified by certain naturally defective persons, and by madmen and drunkards. Therefore it is no wonder that devils can, with God's permission, chain up the reason; and such men are called delirious, because their senses have been snatched away by the devil." [31] Needless to say, under these circumstances a differential diagnosis based on objective data, such as symptoms or signs, was only of an academic value, since a complete confession was the most decisive factor in the whole process of investigation, and any statement of one's delusions and hallucinations was credited as a valid confession. The two honest Dominicans admit, however, that "we have often learned from the confessions of those whom we have caused to be burned, that they have not been willing agents of witchcraft." The problem is best outlined by the authors themselves: "And if it is asked how it is possible to distinguish whether an illness is caused by witchcraft or by some natural physical defect, we answer that there are various methods. And the first is by means of the judgment of doctors. See the words of S. Augustine *On the Christian Doctrine:* To this class of superstition belong all

[31] *Ibid.*, p. 50.

charms and amulets suspended or bound about the person, which the School of Medicine despises. For example, doctors may perceive from the circumstances, such as the patient's age, healthy complexion, and the reaction of his eyes, that his disease does not result from any defect of the blood or the stomach, or any other infirmity; and they therefore judge that it is not due to any natural defect, but to some extrinsic cause. And since that extrinsic cause cannot be any poisonous infection, which would be accompanied by ill humours in the blood and stomach, they have sufficient reason to judge that it is due to witchcraft.

" And secondly, when the disease is incurable, so that the patient can be relieved by no drugs, but rather seems to be aggravated by them.

" Thirdly, the evil may come so suddenly upon a man that it can only be ascribed to witchcraft. An example of how this happened to one man has been made known to us. A certain well-born citizen of Spires had a wife who was of such an obstinate disposition that, though he tried to please her in every way, yet she refused in nearly every way to comply with his wishes, and was always plaguing him with abusive taunts. It happened that, on going into his house one day, and his wife railing against him as usual with opprobrious words, he wished to go out of the house to escape from quarrelling. But she quickly ran before him and locked the door by which he wished to go out; and loudly swore that, unless he beat her, there was no honesty or faithfulness in him. At these heavy words he stretched out his hand, not intending to hurt her, and struck her lightly with his open palm on the buttock; whereupon he suddenly fell to the ground and lost all his senses, and lay in bed for many weeks afflicted with a most grievous illness. Now it is obvious that this was not a natural illness, but was caused by some witchcraft of the woman. And very many similar cases have happened, and been made known to many." [32]

Whatever other keen considerations the *Malleus* may give in connection with the problem of diagnosis, the above statements are the most complete. However, especial attention ought to be drawn to the problem of curability of the affliction. In other words, great suddenness, but particularly chronicity was considered pathognomonic of the work of the devil. The reasoning is as follows: "It is further argued that S. Thomas and S. Bonaventura, in Book IV,

[32] *Ibid.*, p. 87.

dist. 34, have said that a bewitchment must be permanent because it can have no human remedy; for if there is a remedy, it is either unknown to men or unlawful. And these words are taken to mean that this infirmity is incurable and must be regarded as permanent; and they add that, even if God should provide a remedy by coercing the devil, and the devil should remove his plague from a man, and the man should be cured, that cure would not be a human one. Therefore, unless God should cure it, it is not lawful for a man himself to try in any way to look for a cure." [33] This injunction and extreme submissive fatalism with regard to mental diseases was not created or monopolized by the fifteenth century or by the authors of the *Malleus*. In one form or another it continued through the centuries to our day in the form of therapeutic nihilism, custodial care as a substitute for more active therapy, and similar methods of treatment. Evidently we are dealing here with some fundamental attitude of man towards mental disease which requires further and deeper psychological and historical investigation.

To return for a moment to the problem of differential diagnosis: the question was more frequently

[33] *Ibid.*, p. 156.

asked than answered by the authors of the *Malleus*. Therefore, they go into even such a detail as the differentiation between a bewitchment, a demono-pathy, and a real mental illness, a frenzy, i. e., a psychosis. No answer is given. They merely state: "And it need not seem wonderful that devils can do this, when even a natural defect is able to effect the same result, as is shown in the case of frantic and melancholy men, and in maniacs and some drunkards, who are unable to discern truly. For frantic men think they see marvellous things, such as beasts and other horrors, when in actual fact they see nothing." [34] However, this knowledge of classical psychiatry which is reflected in the above quotation, appears to have been book knowledge rather than clinical, for nowhere in the *Malleus* do we find any practical hint as to how to differentiate between the diseases mentioned in the Galenic nosology and the diseases which the Inquisitors describe as machina-tions of witches. We find instead a rather complete knowledge of the symptomatology of mental dis-eases which they use exclusively for purposes of detecting witches. They knew of the hysterical anesthesias which they carefully investigated by

[34] *Ibid.*, p. 120.

means of torture, and through the same means they elicited the phenomenon of extreme pathological mutism, which is so frequently found among stuporous catatonic schizophrenias. They speak of various contortions of the body — evidently hysterical convulsions. Strikingly enough, these are mentioned almost casually. Apparently this type of extreme " Grande Hystérie " did not make its full appearance until later, particularly towards the middle of the sixteenth century, and was dubbed in later centuries hystero-epilepsy (French writers) or hystero-demonopathy (Italian writers). In brief, Sprenger and Kraemer described literally every single type of neurosis or psychosis which we find today in our daily psychiatric work. However, let us go back to the question of the physiological psychology, or the psycho-pathology of the *Malleus*.

7

Did the two Inquisitors resort to any new psycho-physiological theories which would harmonize with their mystico-materialistic concept of the devil's activities? We must answer this question in the negative. They relied primarily on the Thomistic psychology of the " Faculties," and this was naturally

combined with an eclectic, humoral, composite physiology of Galen and Aristotle. To the devil they
relegated the domain of " local motion," i. e., those
invisible changes which would take place within
given organs without affecting the total organism.
The devil could not invade the soul, as only God
could enter there, but he could " enter " any other
part of the organism, including the head, and could
thus affect one's reason. They devote a great deal
of time and space to the consideration of sexual
disorders, such as impotence and perversions, delusions of somatic loss, particularly the loss of sexual
organs, and they speculate with much acumen on
whether a delusion of the loss of a member is a
glamour and a disturbance of the inner or outer
senses, or whether it presents actual organic pathology. The latter is denied, for the devil has no
power beyond his influence on local motion. Auditory hallucinations are discussed in the following
manner: " But since they have understanding, and
when they wish to express their meaning, then, by
some disturbance of the air included in their assumed
body, not of air breathed in and out as in the case
of men, they produce, not voices, but sounds which
have some likeness to voices, and send them articu-

lately through the outside air to the ears of the hearer. And that the likeness of a voice can be made without the respiration of air is clear from the case of other animals which do not breathe, but are said to make a sound, as do also certain other instruments, as Aristotle says in the *De anima.* For certain fishes, when they are caught, suddenly utter a cry outside the water, and die." [35] The *Malleus* never forgets, of course, to make clear that such mental pathology is impossible without sin: "All who are deluded this way are presumed to be in deadly sin" for "as is clear from the words of S. Anthony: The devil can in no way enter the mind or body of any man, nor has the power to penetrate into the thoughts of anybody, unless such a person has first become destitute of all holy thoughts, and is quite bereft and denuded of spiritual contemplation." [36]

One of the greatest difficulties of the time which the *Malleus* had to cope with was the increasing influence of astrological views and fantasies. Somehow it was necessary to bring the *Malleus* into a certain state of harmony with the various trends: a proper place had to be preserved for the lunatic, a proper significance retained for the stars, and

[35] *Ibid.,* p. 110. [36] *Ibid.,* p. 120.

yet while not depriving the devil of his influence, he was not to be endowed with any authority over the astral bodies which were under the direct control of the Lord. To quote the *Malleus:* ". . . there are two reasons why devils molest men at certain phases of the Moon. First, that they may bring disrepute on a creature of God, namely, the Moon, as S. Jerome and S. John Chrysostom say. Secondly, because they cannot, as has been said above, operate except through the medium of the natural powers. Therefore they study the aptitudes of bodies for receiving an impression; and because, as Aristotle says, the brain is the most humid of all the parts of the body, therefore it chiefly is subject to the operation of the Moon, which itself has power to incite humours. Moreover, the animal forces are perfected in the brain, and therefore the devils disturb a man's fancy according to certain phases of the Moon, when the brain is ripe for such influences."[37] And "For certain men who are called Lunatics are molested by devils more at one time than at another; and the devils would not so behave, but would rather molest them at all times, unless they themselves were deeply affected by certain

[37] *Ibid.*, p. 40.

phases of the Moon. It is proved again from the fact that Necromancers observe certain constellations for the invoking of devils, which they would not do unless they knew that those devils were subject to the stars." [38] References are made to the wetness or dryness of the brain, and to the various humors affected in various psychopathic states.

An excellent definition of projection is given: " For fancy or imagination is as it were the treasury of ideas received through the senses. And through this it happens that devils so stir up the inner perceptions, that is the power of conserving images, that they appear to be a new impression at that moment received from exterior things." [39]

Illusions are differentiated from hallucinations. Even the most modern present-day views, establishing an intimate relationship between projections and hallucinations, are duly represented in the *Malleus*, although couched in the heavy-footed phraseology of the fifteenth century:

" The apparitions that come in dreams to sleepers proceed from the ideas retained in the repository of their mind, through a natural local motion caused by the flow of blood to the first and inmost seat of their

[38] *Ibid.*, p. 31.   [39] *Ibid.*, p. 50.

faculties of perception; and we speak of an intrinsic local motion in the head and cells of the brain.

" And this can also happen through a similar local motion created by devils. Also such things happen not only to the sleeping, but even to those who are awake. For in these also the devils can stir up and excite the inner perceptions and humours, so that ideas retained in the respositories of their minds are drawn out and made apparent to the faculties of fancy and imagination, so that such men imagine these things to be true. And this is called interior temptation.

" And it is no wonder that the devil can do this by his own natural power; since any man by himself, being awake and having the use of his reason, can voluntarily draw from his repositories the images he has retained in them; in such a way that he can summon to himself the images of whatsoever things he pleases. And this being granted, it is easy to understand the matter of excessive infatuation in love." [40]

Speaking of love, Sprenger and Kraemer follow the age-long tradition which originated in Greek clinical psychopathology, and which was highly use-

[40] *Ibid.*, p. 50.

ful to their uncompromising ascetic philosophy. They consider love a form of mental illness and invoke the authority of Avicenna to prove that it is an abnormal state of mind. Then on their own, they proceed to link up this mental illness with the devil, since the devil is supposed to have particular power over the business of love — his domain *par excellence*, not so much because of the natural filthiness of the act, as the *Malleus* puts it, but because this was the original sin of our original parents, and the devil continued uninterruptedly in this field ever since the fall of Adam and Eve. Therefore the *Malleus* is firmly convinced that " All witchcraft comes from carnal lust, which is in women insatiable. See *Proverbs* xxx: There are three things that are never satisfied, yea, a fourth thing which says not, It is enough; that is, the mouth of the womb. Wherefore for the sake of fulfilling their lusts they consort even with devils." [41]

Examples are given of systematized delusions similar to those that occur in present-day schizophrenias.

" We Inquisitors had credible experience of this method in the town of Breisach in the diocese of Basel, receiving full information from a young girl witch who had been converted, whose aunt also had

---

[41] *Ibid.*, p. 47.

been burned in the diocese of Strasburg. And she added that she had become a witch by the method in which her aunt had first tried to seduce her.

"For one day her aunt ordered her to go upstairs with her, and at her command to go into a room where she found fifteen young men clothed in green garments after the manner of German knights. And her aunt said to her: Choose whom you wish from these young men, and I will give him to you, and he will take you for his wife. And when she said she did not wish for any of them, she was sorely beaten and at last consented, and was initiated according to the aforesaid ceremony. She said also that she was often transported by night with her aunt over vast distances, even from Strasburg to Cologne." [42]

"Here is another example from the same source. There was lately a general report, brought to the notice of Peter the Judge in Boltingen, that thirteen infants had been devoured in the State of Berne; and public justice exacted full vengeance on the murderers. And when Peter asked one of the captive witches in what manner they ate children, she replied: 'This is the manner of it. We set our snares chiefly for unbaptized children, and even for those

[42] *Ibid.*, p. 100.

57

that have been baptized, especially when they have not been protected by the sign of the Cross and prayers' (Reader, notice that, at the devil's command, they take the unbaptized chiefly, in order that they may not be baptized), 'and with our spells we kill them in their cradles or even when they are sleeping by their parents' side, in such a way that they afterwards are thought to have been overlain or to have died some other natural death. Then we secretly take them from their graves, and cook them in a cauldron, until the whole flesh comes away from the bones to make a soup which may easily be drunk. Of the more solid matter we make an unguent which is of virtue to help us in our arts and pleasures and our transportations; and with the liquid we fill a flask or skin, whoever drinks from which, with the addition of a few other ceremonies, immediately acquires much knowledge and becomes a leader in our sect.' '' [43]

Suicides among witches (through hanging) are reported. In brief, the *Malleus Maleficarum* might with a little editing serve as an excellent modern textbook of descriptive clinical psychiatry of the fifteenth century, if the word *witch* were substituted by the word *patient*, and the devil eliminated.

[43] *Ibid.*, pp. 100-101.

It must be said, however, that although the clinical pictures in general seem similar to those of the present day, the trends — cannibalistic, mystic, delusionary fancies of being possessed by the devil — are the outstanding characteristic of that historical period. As Esquirol pointed out more than a century ago, the mentally sick center their delusionary trends around some outstanding feature of their age — in the fifteenth and sixteenth centuries it was the devil, in the eighteenth century the Jacobins or the Bourbons, and in the nineteenth century the police.

8

As has been said before, the outstanding trend of the *Malleus* is anti-erotic. In some respects it is a textbook of sexual psychopathies. The question naturally arises: why is it that the phenomenon of Inquisition was given by history the extraordinary opportunity to conquer such an immense field of human knowledge and create an "endemic paranoia" for a period of over two centuries? More than one lecture based on profound and special study would be required to envisage an adequate hypothesis. Reference was made above to the thirteenth century and to certain similarities between that period and the Renaissance. It would seem that outside the many and complex economic and political factors which made it necessary for the Church to straighten its ranks and struggle for the maintenance of unity (this meant first of all unity of dogma), a set of psychological factors was released which are of especial interest to us as medical men, particularly to those of us interested in psychopathology.

The Renaissance of Arts and Sciences carried with it an enormous release of human instinctual life. This release was naturally accompanied by a strong biological drive for instinctual self-assertion, for freedom in the broadest possible sense. Such a comparatively sudden awakening of human instincts had to come face to face with the ascetic tradition which had been ruling the world for over a thousand years. When Cassiodorus retired to Monte Casino to live with his books instead of the politicians of Theodoric, the trend was away from the world and away from everything that reminded one of human instincts, human passions, human desires. The latter were rejected, but since instinctual drives cannot be killed, they were projected into the outside world as something evil and represented as the devil. In a sense, everyone who thus turned

away from the world deserved the name given to
St. Benedict — *effugator daemonum* — for he chased
away devils. This tradition was to a great extent
broken, or at any rate it had sustained a severe
shock, by Sprenger and Kraemer's time. What are
traditionally called morals were at a very low ebb,
and a severe conflict had arisen between traditional
authority, which happened at that time to be ascetic,
and the increasing hedonism of the age. The result
was both natural and inevitable — a severe paranoid
psychosis.

It is interesting from this point of view to read
in the *Malleus Maleficarum* the various confessions of, or observations on, the trends of many
witches. "Here it is to be noted that, as has already
been hinted, this iniquity has small and scant beginnings, as that at the time of the elevation of the
Body of Christ they spit on the ground, or shut their
eyes, or mutter some vain words. We know a woman
who yet lives, protected by the secular law, who,
when the priest at the celebration of the Mass blesses
the people, saying, *Dominus uobiscum,* always adds
to herself these words in the vulgar tongue, 'Kehr
mir die Zung im Arss umb.' Or they even say some
such thing at confession after they have received

absolution, or do not confess everything, especially mortal sins, and so by slow degrees are led to a total abnegation of the Faith, and to the abominable profession of sacrilege." [44] In other words, these " witches " were *actually* heretical; they actually

Making a pact with the devil
(A woodcut in the *Compendium Maleficarum*—XVII century)

sinned against the Sacraments, they actually murmured profanities in the churches, and they actually either rebelled against or were afraid of the sign of the Cross — all this while mentally sick, of course. In the light of present-day psychopathology,

[44] *Ibid.*, p. 96.

it is not very difficult to see that we are dealing here mostly, not with hysterias, but with compulsion neuroses and schizophrenic psychoses. It is known that in adolescents and in adults one of the most typical phases of a compulsion neurosis even today is a conscious or unconscious expression of sacrilege, as it were, a series of impulses directed against God, Christ, and the Church. Whatever the psychological reasons for this clinical phenomenon, it is observed today even in our comparatively irreligious and materialistic age. In the fifteenth century, according to the descriptions found in the *Malleus*, it could not have been essentially different. The question as to why medicine seemed to have been swamped or driven into retreat before such a mass of psychiatric material is difficult to answer at present.

The purpose of this lecture, Ladies and Gentlemen, has been primarily to describe and to outline some of the forces at play, rather than to judge, approve or disapprove. I could follow Quintilian by saying *Scribitur ad narrandum non ad probandum*, for the problem is scientific and clinical rather than moral. If I may venture, in conclusion, to skip for a moment the matter to be dealt with in the next two lectures and make a forecast — necessarily nebulous, of course, — as to what the general outcome of this struggle between instinct, civilization, and authority was and some day might be, I would have to join with the witches of Macbeth:

First witch: "When shall we three meet again;
                          In thunder, lightning or in rain?
Second witch: When hurlyburly's done
                          When the battle's lost and won."

A wizard practicing his incantations in Virginia

(After an etching by Theodore de Bry)

LECTURE TWO

MEDICINE AND THE WITCH IN THE SIXTEENTH CENTURY *

1

Ladies and Gentlemen:

The witches' repast
(After Ulrich Molitor's
Landis)

IN the Bibliothèque Nationale in Paris there is preserved, under number 24122, a small manuscript written piously in the year of our Lord, 1591. This manuscript is kept in a parchment folder of a later date and bears the following inscription: "The original of the records (*procès verbal*) of the Court held to deliver a girl who was possessed by an evil spirit in Louvier, in which one will find ample proof of a person being genuinely possessed by a demon." It was published in its original form in 1883 by the Progrès Médical under the direction of Armand Bénet, an authority on old French documents, together with a long introduction by B. de Moray.

* Some of the material related in this lecture will appear also in the *Bulletin* of the New York Academy of Medicine.

The manuscript was written by the not too literate hand of a sixteenth century scribe, Vauquet, under the direction and supervision of the provost of Louvier, Morel, the chief magistrate of this small town in Normandy. The first entry was made on Saturday, the seventeenth of August, 1591, and the last on the fifth of September of the same year. In other words, the trial of Françoise Fontaine — a young girl in her early twenties — required almost three weeks and claimed the constant cooperation and vigilance of the clergy, the attorney of the King, the surgeon Baugeoys Gautier, the physician Roussel, not to mention various lieutenants, specially assigned archers, and the whole population of the town, both Catholic and Protestant (*de la nouvelle prétendue religion*), as well as the inmates of the town prison.

The story, as one is able to cull it from the meticulous descriptions of the proceedings, is to us neither new nor particularly striking. Françoise Fontaine was apparently seduced by someone whom she had never known, while she lived in Paris and worked as a servant. Subsequently, she developed convulsions, auditory hallucinations, and ideas of reference. She believed herself to be possessed by the devil and although she did cooperate, as we would put it today, with her judges and priests, she was not able to "confess," nor was she able to overcome the domination of the devil. She had repeated convulsive attacks in the presence of the Court as well as in church. Offered the Holy Communion, she stood the consecration of the Sacrament well, but at the exact moment when the Host was proffered and she was ready to accept it, the devil broke one of the window panes over the very altar and poor Françoise fell again into one of her malignant, sinful swoons. She was not delivered until the hair from her head and armpits had been shaven by the surgeon who himself was thoroughly frightened and, thrice begging to be excused from performing the task, finally had to be threatened by the provost with severe punishment in the name of His Majesty the King. Following the removal of the hair from her armpits, Françoise appeared to have improved so much that the Court did not deem it necessary to insist on the removal of her pubic hair. She was then turned over to the care of Curé Houdemare, Chaplain Buisson, and two special male guards. She remained in the church for six weeks, receiving Holy Communion daily. Following this, she was "paroled" to the custody of a good lady by the name of Marguérite

Coquette. Although still tormented by the evil spirit, she felt better and twenty months later the lady custodian reported to the provost that Françoise was fully delivered from the devil. However, the conscientious official, much in the manner of a modern psychiatrist, kept a distant watch on her and also a follow-up record, as it were; he related what her occupations were, he recorded the names of her employers in their chronological order, and he catalogued her conduct until he was finally convinced that a good job had been done. The concluding sentence of the record reads: "And after the said Françoise finally left these parts, a priest of the said town of Louvier told us that the above-named Françoise had confessed to him that the said evil spirit called himself Barabas, and that this was the name he gave as his to the above-named Françoise; this she confessed to the above-mentioned priest, who came and duly informed us of the fact." The last installment of the report is signed by " L. Morel, Bellet, M. Pelet, Vauquet, Jehan Buysson, priest, and J. Vymont," i. e., the provost himself, the scribe, the priest, and other attachés. There is no signature of a physician.

As we have said, the story presents no striking features. It merely adds another to a mass of hundreds of thousands, if not millions, of similar cases which were observed in those days, and which some Italian psychiatrists of the nineteenth century skilfully dubbed *hystero-demonopathies.* However, the manuscript is interesting for its genuineness and for the local color it offers. Its homely, naïvely crude, and not less naïvely frank narrative relates how the candles were blown out in the midst of the court session, supposedly by the devil, and how the assisting priest pulled out a dagger ready to attack the assaulting devil. It tells us how one night in the town prison Françoise developed a severe excitement, later threw herself head foremost into the well, was caught by some obstacle half-way down, and remained suspended; how the peaceful inmates of the prison calmly left the prison and went to report to the provost — they appeared to have been the only ones who were not very frightened — and in the small hours of the morning the scared, trembling chief magistrate of the town marched to the prison under the protective guard of his own prisoners who received a generous reward of wine and money for their good deed.

It would be idle, of course, to try to subject to modern scrutiny the symptoms of Françoise Fontaine in order to prove the obvious fact that she was a mentally sick girl. It is far more interesting to try to establish what the attitude of the medical man in such cases was, and why his attitude was what it was. We cannot very well dispose of the problem by reiterating the traditional statement that those were centuries of dark ignorance and of cruel domination by a superstitious Church. A century that gave us scientists such as Tycho Brahe, Regio Montanus, Telesius, Erasmus, Melanchton, Vives, Cornelius Agrippa, Cardanus, Nicolaus Cusanus, among others, could hardly be thought of as ignorant. The names mentioned did not belong to atheists, but were borne by devoutly religious men both Catholic and Protestant. On the other hand, one can hardly speak of the medical profession of the sixteenth century as one of ignorance, as it was that century that gave us such anatomists as Vesalius, Fallopius (died in 1562), Eustachius (died in 1574), and also Servetus, the discoverer of the pulmonary circulation (burned in 1553). The sixteenth century also gave us such clinicians as Girolamo Fracastorius (infectious disease and syphilis); Jean Fernel; Felix Plater; Paracelsus; the father of modern surgery, Ambroise Paré; the great plastic surgeon from Bologna, Gaspare

Tagliacozzo; Johann Weyer, of whom we will speak in the concluding lecture; and last but not least, Francis Bacon, whose influence on medical thought must not be overlooked any more than the destructive banter of Rabelais or the searching and penetrating irony of Montaigne. This very brief list of names alone should convince us that the sixteenth century had quite thoroughly assimilated the knowledge of the Greco-Roman past, and proceeded with a great deal of searching curiosity to develop a serious scientific foundation for the future. It was therefore by no means ignorant, nor was it lacking — considering its scientific resources — in that skepticism and critical spirit without which scientific work is impossible. It did look for facts, it did try to master facts, and it was slowly learning to respect facts.

In one regard, however, the sixteenth century, like its predecessor, continued to lag behind, and it did so for at least another three centuries, apparently unable to cast off the fetter of tradition — it was as yet unprepared even to begin to develop a sound medical psychology. As was pointed out with some detail in the first lecture and in a previous communication,[1] there were many factors

[1] Zilboorg, Gregory, " The Dark Ages of Psychiatric History,"

interfering with clear vision. That the Church was the chief bearer of the tradition which believed superstitiously in the devil, sorcerers, witches, and their satellites, there is no doubt; but there is also no less doubt that this tradition was rather borne than inspired by the Church, who neither created nor abolished it. As has been alluded to in the first lecture, we deal here apparently with a tradition deeply rooted in man's own psychology from the dawn of his life on earth, and from which we are not entirely free even today. While today we laugh at ourselves, so to speak, when we knock ·on wood, avoid a black cat on the road, dislike Friday, or are suspicious of the thirteenth, we do nevertheless still knock on wood, avoid a black cat, fear a broken mirror, and dislike the thirteenth. We may recall that the Reverend Montague Summers, of whom we spoke in the first lecture, actually still believes that witches and sorcerers were incontestable realities and that they were " a well-organized international unit bent on destroying civilization, a dark fraternity just as the Third International, the Anarchists, the Nihilists, and the Bolsheviks." [2]

The Journal of Nervous and Mental Disease, Vol. 74, No. 5, November, 1931.

[2] Summers, Rev. Montague, *op. cit.*, p. xviii.

While the sixteenth century was apparently as yet unprepared to make a clear step in the direction of a sound medical psychology, there was no dearth of clinical material. The illustrative examples cited in the *Malleus Maleficarum* bear witness to this. Moreover, the medical literature of the nineteenth century collected a number of data which it subjected to such careful clinical scrutiny that no doubt is left in our mind that the millions of witches, sorcerers, possessed and obsessed, were an enormous mass of severe neurotics, psychotics, and considerably deteriorated organic deliria. In the two volumes of Calmeil [3] alone one can find a valuable collection of such material, and the comparative study of B. de Moray [4] would also suffice as a convincing clinical analysis. At times one is almost loath to admit to one's self the indisputable fact that for many years the world looked like a veritable insane asylum without a proper mental hospital. The words of Judge Boguet give most flagrant contemporaneous support to our contention. Boguet, a judge in Burgundy in the days of Henry IV, made the following speech at the dedication of the Abbé d'Acey, a speech which

[3] Calmeil, L.-F., *De La Folie*, 2 vols. (Paris, 1845).

[4] Moray, B. de, Introduction to the manuscript referred to above (Paris, 1883).

73

was subsequently printed: "I believe that the sorcerers could form an army equal to that of Xerxes who had one million, eight hundred thousand men. Trois-Echelles, one of those best acquainted with the craft of sorcerers, states that under King Charles IV, France alone had three hundred thousand sorcerers (some read it as thirty thousand). This being the case, what should we estimate the total number to be if we include other countries and regions of the world? Are we not justified in believing that since those days the number has increased at least by half? As to myself, I have no doubts, since a mere glance at our neighbors will convince us that the land is infested with this unfortunate and damnable vermin. Germany cannot do anything else but raise fires against them; Switzerland is compelled to do likewise, thus depopulating many of its villages; Lorraine reveals to a visitor thousands and thousands of poles to which the sorcerers are tied; and as to ourselves, who are not exempt from this trouble any more than others are, we are witnessing a number of executions in various parts of the land. Now to return to our neighbors, Savoie is not yet emptied, since she sends us daily an infinite number of people possessed by devils who, when conjured up, tell us that they were put into the bodies of those poor people by sorcerers. Adding to this the fact that the principal ones whom we have burned here in Burgundy came originally from there, what judgment could we form of France? It is difficult to believe that she will ever be purged, given the great number that she had in the days of Trois-Echelles, let alone other more outlying regions. No, no, the sorcerers reach everywhere by the thousands; they multiply on this earth like the caterpillars in our gardens. . . . I want them to know that if the results would correspond with my wishes, the earth would be quickly purged because I wish they could all be united in one body so that they all could be burned on one fire." [5] This inflammatory but very sincere speech voiced a belief and a desire common to millions. The fiery and panicky state of the majority of people generated more and more evil spirits, so that towards the latter part of the sixteenth century the enlightened Johann Weyer compiled, from books and observations, the total number of demons and evil spirits which he estimated to be 7,405,926, commanded over by seventy-two " Princes of Darkness." [6] A possessed individual was not necessarily

[5] Quoted by Calmeil, Vol. I, pp. 216-217.
[6] Wierus, Joanes, *Pseudomonarchia Daemonum*, 1577.

inhabited by one single spirit; several, even many, could enter one human body. Thus it was reported that St. Fortunatus cured a man who was possessed by 6,670 evil spirits.[7] Without going into any of the intricacies of the theoretical superstructure which supported the convictions we are dealing with, it can be stated that the devil's favorite mode of contact with the human body was that of sexual congress. This was a fact which a Cardinal once stated one would be impudent not to believe: *idque negari non posse absque impudentia.*[8]

What was the attitude of the learned men of the day who dared to doubt these assumptions? At first, particularly in the fifteenth century, they became interested in those things which were as distant from theology as possible; they treated these flagrant but unapproachable problems with the "eloquence of silence."[9] Speaking about Telesius, an historian

[7] Moray, B. de, *op. cit.*, p. lix.

[8] *Multis experimentis compertum est, interdum mulieribus improbos esse dæmones, earumque concubitum expetere et peragere, idque negari non posse absque impudentia.* Moray, B. de, *op. cit.*, p. lxix. This anonymous Cardinal was apparently reiterating the words of St. Augustine, which were quoted by the *Malleus* and cited in the first lecture.

[9] The expression is Brett's. Cf. Brett, George: *History of Psychology*, 3 vols. (London, 1921). Vol. I, p. 160.

summarizes the method as follows: "Thus in man there are two kinds of spirits, two distinct agencies, not merely a soul united with matter, but material spirits, and something of higher nature. The latter can be ignored while we consider the corporeal life of man and so drops out of all consideration. This was the standard method of avoiding the theological part of the doctrine of man."[10] This is the reason why Daremberg felt justified in saying that the fifteenth century was both active and sterile — both a summary and a preface. It was active because people were very busy unearthing, translating, reading, and studying the rediscovered ancient texts. It was sterile because they failed to do much thinking of their own. It was a summary of the past and a preface to the great advances made in the sixteenth century. Not until the end of the sixteenth century, however, did the actual text of scientific doubt, to which the previous century was a preface, begin to be written. The cautious silence of Telesius stands out in striking contrast to Montaigne's incisive laughter. It is Montaigne who says: "Through presumptions they make laws for nature and marvel at the way nature ignores those laws."

[10] Brett, George, *op. cit.*, Vol. I, p. 146.

In the meantime the whole field of clinical psychiatry was covered by theologians whose psychiatric practice seemed to emanate almost exclusively from the twenty-seventh verse of the twentieth chapter of Leviticus. The verse reads: "A man also, or woman, that hath a familiar spirit, or that is a wizard, shall surely be put to death: they shall stone them with stones; their blood *shall be* upon them."

2

If we return now to the story of Françoise Fontaine, we shall find that even a cursory perusal of the text will impress us with the earnestness and honesty of those who were in charge of the trial. They were at times frightened, at times angered, but on the whole they treated Françoise with consideration, and they were eager to give her the full benefit of the doubt. We thus find that " Because we heard it said that in order to prevent a sorcerer from doing evil, it was necessary to obtain a new broom made of birch wood and to beat with it the said sorcerer, and fearing lest the above-said Françoise be a sorceress, since we saw that what she was doing was something supernatural and beyond human ken, we demanded that a new broom be produced. This was brought to us from the jail; we beat the said Françoise with this broom and hit her on the body several times, doing which, however, we used up the broom before the said Françoise came to." [11] The girl failed to recover with this treatment. We may add parenthetically that the contemporary theory was that stupors and stupor-like states were due to the fact that a dumb or deaf-and-dumb evil spirit had entered the person. A stuporous state did not even profit exemption from the accusation that the afflicted one attended the Witches' Sabbath -- the spirit attended, while the body lay as if dead in bed. However that may be, Françoise was brought to consciousness for a few minutes, and was able to make five or six steps to enter the court-room. At that moment, the doctor and the surgeon, named Roussel and Gautier respectively, made their entry and were informed of what had happened heretofore. All this occurred on August 31, 1591, exactly fourteen days after the opening of the trial. As we see, a medical opinion was not considered a very urgent matter, although it was not cast off as altogether unnecessary. In the meantime, Françoise had fallen to the floor, experiencing a second or a re-

[11] *Procès Verbal, etc.*, pp. 28-29.

entrance to her first spell. The doctor and the surgeon " saw that the neck of the said Françoise was quite swollen and that she threw herself here and there; they were as astonished as we were and the said Roussel (the physician) stated that he was in possession of the root of a certain herb, the name of which he gave us but which we have forgotten,[12] and he said that if he put it in the mouth of the said Françoise he would be able to say whether it was a sickness or an evil spirit that possessed her. We at once dragged the body of the said Françoise, she remaining on her back, along the said court-room — which procedure was observed by the said Roussel, the doctor, who according to his own statement belonged to the new alleged religion. He then stated that the said Françoise was possessed by an evil spirit and that it was beyond his power to prescribe anything for her." During this time Françoise continued to " lie on the floor face upward, arms extended like a cross, squirming in all directions." [13]

From this moment on, the procedure turned into the direction of traditional exorcisms and other authorized ecclesiastic methods of casting out the

[12] The *Malleus Maleficarum* refers to such an herb, but its botanical name is lacking; it is called " demonofuge."
[13] *Procès Verbal, etc.*, p. 30.

devil. One might be inclined to consider as atypical the behaviour of the small town physician, Roussel, but this assumption cannot be entirely borne out by facts. One might also wonder what the views of those of his colleagues were who had had the benefit of living in large cities and great centers of learning. All traditions die hard and the medical tradition of keeping away from the devil's tricks died perhaps the hardest. Even the anatomical discoveries of Vesalius, which could be so easily demonstrated on the cadaver, did not at first appear convincing to his contemporaries. They were more ready to assume that the discrepancies between Galen and Vesalius were due to the fact that humanity had degenerated since the days of Galen, than to admit that the great physician of Pergamos was wrong. As a matter of fact, the teacher of Vesalius himself, Jacques Dubois (Sylvius), thought that Vesalius was "crazy." [14] Moreover, the influence of public opinion could not help but exert its pressure on the medical profession in a manner both effective and deadening.

We must not forget that even the enlightened humanist Melanchton sent a congratulatory letter to Calvin soon after learning that Servetus had been

[14] Diepgen, Paul, *Geschichte der Medizin*, 5 vols. (Berlin, 1913-28). Vol. III, p. 14.

righteously burned at the stake. The medical profession on the whole was unable, until the very end of the century, to surmise that some day it might want to have and even be called upon to do something with the host of alleged possessed, sorcerers, demonomaniacs, and bewitched. We may well omit consideration of the great lay authorities who dwelt on the devil and his deviltries. Such keen and ingenious minds as Jean Bodin, for instance, devoted a great deal of time and energy to the study of what Montaigne called "presumptions through which they made laws of nature." Their duty and historical function was, through the very nature of their task, to preserve and not to let go, to codify and not to rescind, to justify the belief rather than to test it. As to the medical clinician, he was just beginning to look askance at that phenomenon of demonomania about which, until now, he had not even dared to wonder. Thus John Lange (1484-1565), one of the most distinguished physicians of his day, states in his *Medicinalium epistolarum miscelanea*,[15] published in 1554: "Ulrich Neussesser, a peasant in Tugenstal, killed himself in 1539 with a sharp tool. A few days before his death an enor-

[15] Quoted from Calmeil, *op. cit.*, Vol. I, p. 174.

mous nail was extracted from Ulrich's abdomen by means of an incision into the skin where the nail protruded. Those who performed an autopsy following the felony (suicide), removed from the stomach an enormous piece of wood, four knives, two pieces of iron, and a bunch of hair." All these objects, they stated, had been deposited there by some diabolical trick. Lange did not hesitate to cite this as an illustration confirming the existence of supernatural diseases; he also quotes the example of a woman who vomited out two iron nails, two needles, and a bunch of hair.[16]

Lange was not an exception, of course. Ambroise Paré, the younger contemporary of Lange, specifically stated in his medical writings that the devil could assume any guise he pleased from serpent to raven, cat, or dog; he could turn over pages in the dark, count money, or throw things about the room at night.

[16] The veracity and oddity of what might be called "pathological swallowers" is not confined to the nineteenth century. There is a collection of very striking radiographs at Bloomingdale Hospital which discloses the swallowing propensities of some depressions and schizophrenias who for a long time before they reached the Hospital successfully practiced the incorporation of numberless hairpins, teaspoons, thermometers, etc. However, while this symptom still persists in the twentieth century, demonomania, like chlorosis or sweating sickness, has all but disappeared.

Once, when attending Court, he observed Charles IX laugh heartily at the tricks shown by a magician. The illustrious surgeon bent over and whispered into His Majesty's ear: "Thou shalt not suffer a witch to live." In his clinical observations, Paré apparently regarded the work of the devil as one of the points to be considered when a differential diagnostic problem presented itself. He thus reported the following:

"From time to time a young nobleman had convulsions which involved different parts of his body such as the left arm, or the right, or on occasion only a single finger, one loin or both, or his spine, and then his whole body would become so suddenly convulsed and disturbed that four servants would have difficulty in keeping him in bed. His brain, however, was in no way agitated or tormented, his speech was free, his mind was not confused, and his sensations, particularly in the regions of the convulsions, remained intact. He was tortured by these convulsions at least twice a day, emerging completely fatigued and broken for they caused him a great deal of torment. Any well-advised physician would have said that we were dealing with a case of genuine epilepsy, were it not for the fact that the senses and mind of the patient

84

remained unaffected throughout the attacks. All the good physicians consulted came to the conclusion that we were dealing here with a convulsion which was the nearest approach to that of epilepsy, that these convulsions must have been provoked by a malignant vapor lodged within the spinal cord, and that because the said vapor expanded into those nerves which originate within the spinal cord only, they failed to affect the brain itself. The cause of the malady was thus established by this judgment and no measure that medical art had at its disposal was forgotten in order to relieve the poor patient of his distress; yet all our efforts remained of no avail since we were miles and miles away from the real cause of the trouble.

"For, at the end of the third month it was discovered that it was the devil who was the cause of the malady. This was learned from a statement made by the devil himself, speaking through the lips of the patient in profuse Latin and Greek. The devil would always discover the secret intentions of those who attended to the patient's needs and particularly the plans of the physicians. He stated with mockery that despite the great danger to his own safety he had succeeded in circumventing all medical procedures.

The physicians thus rendered useless, the patient almost died. Each time the father of the patient came to see his son, the devil would grow impatient and would shout as soon as he saw him at a distance: ' Make him go back; don't let him come in,' or ' Take the chain off his collar.' The father of the patient was a noble knight and, in accordance with the customs of French knights, he wore the collar of his Order from which dangled a chain with the image of Saint Michael. The patient would become restless whenever anyone attempted to read him a passage from the Holy Scriptures. He would try to rise, and would then be even more tormented. The paroxysms over, the poor, sick man would recall everything he had done or said and would repent, saying that he had said and done all these things against his own will.

" This devil, forced to talk frankly by means of religious services and exorcisms, stated that he was a spirit and that he was not at all to be damned for any violation of contract whatsoever. He was then interrogated as to what kind of spirit he was, and by what means and by virtue of what authority he tormented the young nobleman. He replied that he had many residences where he hid himself and that during the time he let our patient rest, he moved about tormenting other people. He also stated that he was relegated to the body of our patient by someone whose name he did not want to give, that he entered it through the patient's feet and went up to the level of the brain, and that he would leave the patient also through the latter's feet but not until the day set by previous agreement had arrived. Following the custom of other servants of the devil, he talked about many other things. I want to assure you that I am not reporting all this merely to play it up as something new, but in order to make people recognize that the devil does enter at times into our bodies and tortures us with unheard of torments. Occasionally he does not enter the body at all, but just agitates the good humors within us, or sends bad humors into the different parts of our bodies." [17]

Nor was Jean Fernel (1497-1558), one of the greatest clinicians of his time, free from the same

[17] Paré, Ambroise, *Oeuvres* (Lyons, 1633). Quoted also by Calmeil, *op. cit.*, pp. 176-178. Weyer, in *De praestigiis daemonum*, Book IV, Chapter XVI, relates the identical case and credits it to Jean Fernel. Weyer is probably correct. Evidently Paré copied this case report from Fernel as he did on some occasions from Nider. It is possible, of course, that both Fernel and Paré "borrowed" the case from one and the same non-identified source. However, whether authentic or plagiarized the quotation remains characteristic of Paré's attitude.

bias. Fernel was a scientist and clinician of the first order — a man who in his spare time amused himself by calculating the size of the earth — but even he followed tradition and, despite contrary clinical evidence, believed in the existence of lycanthropy (werewolves) as a clinical entity. This "disease" was described by the later representatives of Greco-Roman medicine, particularly Celsus and Paulus Aeginatus, and in the sixteenth century, old books frequently exercised a greater influence on the mind of the practicing physician than clinical facts. This explains why Daremberg stated, at the risk of provoking great astonishment, that he found the medical history of the sixteenth century less attractive than that of the fifteenth. "The history of the sixteenth century," says Daremberg, "could be reduced to the following three points: the humanists busy discussing texts; anatomists scrutinizing nature; and Paracelsus dreaming at high noon and raving delirious while in full possession of his senses." [18]

Before we give any details of Paracelsus' "dreams" and "deliria," we might state that the medical man of the sixteenth century, imbued as he was with the

[18] Daremberg, Charles, *Histoire des Sciences Médicales*, 2 vols. (Paris, 1870). Vol. I, p. 355.

physiology of the re-discovered Greco-Roman science, could not help but remain the child of his age. Here and there physicians, great authorities on ancient medicine (Montanus, Schenk, Houllier), did describe clinical conditions similar to those of diabolic possession and did consider them physical — particularly cerebral — affections, but in this they appeared more to follow the noble literary tradition of the Hippocratico-Galenic theory than to raise an effective protest against the prevailing practices. The devil and the witch, his chief servant on earth, remained an entity apart from medicine, and medicine openly and passively accepted the current attitude. For a long time medicine failed either to register a serious protest or to undertake a dispassionate scientific study of the phenomenon of demonolatry. That the witch was a witch no one doubted, but occasionally one heard a reference to what we might today call the physical or constitutional predisposition to possession by the devil; the concept being that the devil needed some weak organ in the human body in order to settle there. This, of course, was not a revolutionary idea,[19] nor was it even new since St. Jerome, who died at the beginning of the fifth century (420), had already

[19] The *Malleus* made explicit reference to this. Cf. Lecture One.

represented this point of view when he said that black bile (atrabile) was the favorite liquid in which the devil loved to bathe. Moreover, as we see from the case cited by Ambroise Paré and from the writings of Fernel and Plater (1536-1614), the devil was apparently free to choose the point of entry and the organ wherein to reside without the prerequisite of anatomical or physiological pathology. So deeply rooted was the concept of the witch in the mind of the clinician that the closest and most conscientious observations and studies did not arouse in him the temerity necessary to subject witchcraft to scientific doubt and the witch to clinical investigation. Plater, a very conscientious and industrious doctor, had two hobbies: he collected musical instruments and he kept company with maniacs, frenetics and the idiots of the town. He not only visited the dungeons where the "insane" were kept, but actually lived there with them for a time, sharing their filth and misery. He was one of the first, if not the first, in modern times to attempt a scientific psychiatric nosology. Yet Plater came from these strenuous, serious studies a firm believer in the devil as the causative agent of many mental conditions which we would today classify as psychoses.

It is for the future historical sociologist to find a definite scientific explanation for the various forces which combined to make the idea of the witch such a tenaciously cruel and almost ineradicable concept in medicine. This communication is concerned only with registering the facts which marked the evolution that medical thought underwent in the course of the sixteenth century. From what has been said, one would be justified in concluding that up to the very close of the century medicine either shied off and away from the problem, or joined hands with public opinion and the jurist in the principle of " Thou shalt not suffer a witch to live," or by way of ineffective compromise followed St. Jerome's views, preserving both the current increasingly scientific anatomy and physiology and the persistent belief in witchcraft. No one seemed ready as yet to recall Canon Timothy's counsel, advising that if a wife be disturbed by an evil spirit she be sent back to her husband who should take her to a doctor to be treated for her craze.[20]

---

[20] Moray, B. de, *op. cit.*, p. xxxvi.

3

We may now return to the "delirium" of Paracelsus. The bombastic Theophrastus was a strange man. A rather disturbed and hectic mind, violent of word, at times disconcerting in behavior — though as violent and as disconcerting in his sincerity even at the height of his conceit — he was the real medical Don Quixote of his age. Were his clinical, scientific ability equal to his uncanny clinical intuition, he would undoubtedly have been the first to disturb the stagnancy of medical psychology. Unfortunately his greatest endowments in this field were temperament (of Paracelsus it is more correct to say temper) and intuition. His interest in mental diseases showed itself very early: he wrote his *De morbis amentium* in 1525 or 1526 (according to Sudhoff) when he was only thirty-one years old and already professor at the University of Basel, although it was not published until after his death, almost forty years later.[21] "Possessions," exclaimed Paracelsus, "while they are not physical diseases, are a definite type of pathological accident. Mental dis-

[21] The Basel German original was used for this study. It is entitled *Medici Aureoli Theophrasti Paracelsi Schreiben / von den Krankheyten / so die Vernunft berauben, etc.* (Basiliae, 1567).

eases have nothing to do with evil spirits or devils; the individuals who are mentally sick merely drink more of the ' astral wine' than they can assimilate; the experienced (doctor) should not study how to exorcise the devil, but rather how to cure the insane. Some mentally sick are animals with sane minds and some are insane animals." "The insane and the sick," Paracelsus says further, " are our brothers, let us give them treatment to cure them for nobody knows whom among our friends or relatives this misfortune may strike." In other words, Paracelsus was violently outspoken against the views of his contemporaries and preached a new psychiatry. He belonged to what Daremberg called " the turbulent minority who did not respect the Greeks any more than the Arabs." Daremberg states: " I should gladly call the chief of this faction (Paracelsus) the Luther of medicine, if he had succeeded in something more than in augmenting the ruins of the past, i. e., if he had succeeded in founding something durable and if he himself had not said that Luther was not worthy even of unlacing his shoes." [22]

Like Luther, Paracelsus did not lack in explosive, tempestuous ideas, but unlike him he did lack in suffi-

[22] Daremberg, Charles, *op. cit.*, pp. 325-326.

cient detachment. He was not infrequently moved to be rather cruel and had no use for those mentally sick who did not easily respond to his treatment. They were to him but hopeless animals and he recommended that they be thrown into the darkness of dungeons for the rest of their days. Following his weird physico-chemical theories, he recommended that the bodies of the mentally sick be scarified, especially the tips of their fingers and toes, to form an outlet for the pathogenic fluids and vapors. In other words, the emotions and the theoretical concepts of Paracelsus were revolutionary and rebellious, but he lacked in disciplined thinking and hence had no scientific method. *Mutatis mutandis*, the same might be said of Rabelais and Montaigne who, each in his own way, gave vent to rebellious sarcasm and sardonic dissatisfaction with tradition, but who naturally were unable scientifically to test the illusions of the age which they so persistently combatted. The real scientific battle did not begin until the last quarter of the century, and it was to be waged for a long time to come.

4

Non-medical thought was able to fight only in the manner of Rabelais and Montaigne, that is, with derision. More aggressive methods would naturally have led to the scaffold or the pyre. On the other hand liberal thought, humanistic and humanitarian though it was, was bookish; though it was keen and penetrating, it could not be very influential, since scientific books and treatises could not be very effective mediums only a century after the discovery of the printing press. Moreover, at a time when Europe was literally studded with pyres and scaffolds, a plain and dispassionate statement of fact was not exactly the most efficient weapon to use. That is probably why such clear-thinking men as Juan Luis Vives or Levinus Lemnius (he was a physician) left but little imprint on their generation, no matter how important their writings might be to the historian of European thought.

Vives (1492-1540), interested in things human, made a very serious attempt to reorganize the care of the mentally sick in his native city of Valencia. In his intelligent concern about the psychological problems of man, he appears to have been in more than one respect far ahead of his time. Known primarily as an educator in the history of the later Renaissance and considered by many the founder of feminine education, he is hardly remembered as a psychologist despite the fact that in the third book of his *De anima et vita*, entitled *De affectibus*, he is apparently the first to deal with human affects, and treats the subject with unusual keenness and in a manner quite modern even while continuing the old Aristotelian tradition.[23]

As for Levinus Lemnius (1505-1568), " he recognized that although energumens do improvise and use unknown languages, and although they do at times appear to know temporarily a tongue which they have never been taught, they possess this faculty while in a state of ecstasy that is attributable to vehement cerebral stimulation: the humors viciated by the malady exercise an influence on the brain as strong as heady wine, or they act in the same way as a blow which arouses sparks from a flint stone, or as a fever which arouses certain forces usually not present in the organs of our body. Spirits and demons have no part in the production of the phenomena mentioned, and therapeutic measures remove them at times quite promptly. At one time epilepsy was also

[23] Vivis, Joannis Lodovici, *De anima et vita libri tres* (Basileae, 1538).

attributed to the activity of maleficent spirits, but it is no longer considered a supernatural affection. It is in the brain and in the humors that one should look for the cause of those attacks which betray the presence of the falling disease." [24]

Lemnius made a very serious attempt to formulate a purely descriptive psychology and, like many humanists of his day, tried quite early to view the individual from a characteriological point of view. While his formulation might appear to us a bit naïve, it is none the less human as well as characteristic. He thus claimed: " . . . mind and body are both subject to changes due to climate and the different regions of the earth: humours, not evil spirits, cause diseases: even the power of speaking in unknown tongues is not due to possession but to latent memories, for if it were a daemon that spoke from within he might as well go on speaking after the possessed was cured of the disease. The spirit of scientific inquiry shows itself in the remarks of Lemnius on conscience. Conscience, he says, is most effective in the morning: the evil vapours are then removed and the pain of conscience (like a headache) accompanies the memory of sin: to con-

[24] Calmeil, *op. cit.*, Vol. I, p. 189.

fess the sin is to gain relief, for feeling, if pent up, corrupts the humours of the body: David usually repented in the morning, and he has testified to the good results. Conscience is very dependent on one's mode of life and one's complexion or constitution: sailors, innkeepers, tightrope walkers, usurers, bankers and small shopkeepers usually have little conscience: theirs is a busy life. The sedentary and the melancholy, on the other hand, have too much conscience: they foster imaginary sins and repent unnecessarily. The young sin and are not troubled: the sick and the aged magnify their faults and brood over their deeds.

"Lemnius is hardly a classical psychologist, but after the academic disputes of the preceding centuries there is a refreshing clearness and sanity in these observations. For they entirely give up the usual generalizations about the inborn knowledge of the good, and show the variety of human nature and human occupations." [25]

It is quite evident from the above that in their attempt to destroy the superstitious scaffolding of the age, the essayist, the philosopher, and the physician had but little more that was new and convincing

[25] Brett, George, *op. cit.*, Vol. II, p. 140.

HENRICUS CORNELIUS AGRIPPA Med & IC.EQU

*Nafcitur Colon.
Agrip.
Obijt Anno 1535.*

*Stemmate natus Eques, Medicus Magus atq; peritus
Juris et Imperij consul Agrippa fui.*

to offer than was found in the old writings of the Greeks. The argument appears to us both anachronistic and somewhat anemic, no matter how correct it was, for in matters dealing with psychopathology the learned man of the sixteenth century had little more to fall back on than Hippocrates' original humoral theory and his views on the Sacred Disease, expressed two thousand years previously. The medical man struggled against his own deficiency, and towards the close of the century had accumulated sufficient clinical observation to perceive a serious doubt. He was no longer able to be as glib and as garrulous on the matter as was Ambroise Paré twenty-five years earlier, yet he could do nothing but grope for some explanation within the limits of a truly primitive physiology and only an embryonal psychology. Nicolas Lepois can serve as a perfect illustration of this rationalistic groping. Not as great a man as his older brother, whose place he took as the personal physician of Prince Charles of Lorraine, he was nevertheless a great student. In 1580, the year Montaigne first issued his essays, Lepois published a treatise on internal medicine, which survived almost two hundred years, one edition appearing with an introduction by

100

Boerhaave. The problem that stood before psychological medicine, represented by men like Lange and Paré, was how to differentiate between *natural* (i. e., organic) and *supernatural* (i. e., demoniacal) affliction. As will be remembered, they saw little difficulty in the problem. If the patient did not react to a certain herb, if he or she suddenly began to talk an ancient tongue, or said of themselves that they were acting against their own will, or if they described their hallucinatory experiences — the affliction was *not natural.* The trend represented by Lepois was to prove by quotation or speculation that the whole field of demonopathies could be explained on the basis of *natural*, i. e., physical causes. To a large majority of the people the mentally sick person was still guilty by virtue of his sickness and it was not as necessary for a person to prove the patient's guilt, as for the patient to prove his innocence. This was obviously a very difficult problem. Lepois thought that physicians could not justify the belief in demonolatry. While he conceded that there existed a state of mind which might be called the delirium of inspiration caused, according to Plato, by the breath of Apollo and operative in prophets, sibyls, and such, he believed that in medical practice one should not attribute mental disease to the influence of spirits.[26] Lepois also described his various observations on transient, acute, and permanent states of loss of memory, and in every case attributed them to cerebral pathology. However, he had nothing to offer in scientific corroboration of his views, outside of sound clinical observation and profound medical erudition. His statement, therefore, that the brain might be affected directly or " by sympathy " is a reiteration of the old Galenic theory. He could do no more, for medicine was still awaiting the coming of Harvey, Haller, Willis, and Bichat.

5

As we see, the last quarter of the sixteenth century was marked by an increasingly restless doubt, a doubt which crept farther and farther into medical thought. It is clear that man and his humanness, the chief object of interest to the Renaissance, presented the medical man with a psychological problem which was most puzzling, most intricate, and most dangerous. In this respect the sixteenth century appears to be sharply defined from its beginning to its end. It was in 1501, in the first year of the century, that

[26] Calmeil, *op. cit.*, Vol. I, pp. 211-212.

Magnus Hundt published his *Nature of Man*, coin-
ing a new word *anthropologia*, and it was toward
the very close of the century that the restlessness of
medical thought, preoccupied with human problems,
became most marked. Thus some medical men had
radically changed their whole manner of thinking
within a very short span of time. Cornelius Agrippa
(1486-1535), for example, started his career with
a mystical, astrological, and alchemical trend, characteristic of the age, and gained, albeit undeservedly,
the shady reputation of a magician, or even a wizard,
well-versed in this field of " sciences "; towards
the latter part of his life he published a book in
which, beginning with the title itself and continuing
throughout the text, we find an unequivocal denunciation of all the occult sciences of the day, of
all the sophistries, dialectic falsehoods, and religious hypocrisies together with a frank declaration
that all such " sciences " are uncertain and vain.[27]
Agrippa, Doctor of both Faculties and of Medicine, was interested in mental diseases and openly
fought the courts for witch-hunting. Needless to
say, he was looked upon as a questionable and

[27] Agrippae, Henrici Cornelii, *De incertitudine et vanitate scien-
tiarum declamatio invectiva.* Paris (probably 1525).

rather tricky character. Everything about him, even his French poodle dog, was considered suspicious. As a matter of fact, people thought that the dog, whose name was *Monsieur*, was the devil himself, or one of his deputies, under whose guidance Agrippa lived and worked — hence Agrippa called him politely *Monsieur*. Nor did the man escape the suspicions of his more enlightened contemporaries. We find him depicted in Rabelais' highly destructive caricature *Pantagruel* under the name of La Trippa.

Whatever suspicious and fanatical contemporaries may have said against Agrippa, he was a valiant man, an honest doctor, a humanitarian citizen of the world, and one of the real pioneers in combatting the universal psychosis of demonological philosophy. Endowed with a restless personality, Agrippa was not so much a scientific leader as an irascible, stormy fighter with a predilection for a purely frontal attack. Conservative and peaceful by nature, a German nobleman ambitious for court honors and positions, he cherished at the same time the modest and laudable wish to become a professor in a reputable university, and studied incessantly. His inventive mind and vivid imagination imbued him with the most contrasting and self-contradictory trends: he was at the same time a good soldier and a good student; he fought in the ranks but carried books and manuscripts in his military rucksack; he hated turmoil and war, denouncing it most bitterly, but he invented some new machine of destruction (a cannon or a gun) and was eager to sell it to the Emperor; he moved from place to place and from job to job because he was seldom paid for his work, and yet had time to construct an optical instrument with which to observe the stars and was thus at the very threshold of inventing a telescope; he denounced the occult sciences and magic, yet had published his *Occult Philosophy* almost simultaneously with his denunciation of it (*On the Uncertainty and Vanity of All Sciences*). A man of great loyalty and devotion, he was endowed with an unusual capacity for making sincere and loyal friends among the rich and the poor, the vulgar and the learned, the lay and the ecclesiastic; yet he made a host of violent enemies among the very people upon whose favors he depended and whose power threatened to destroy him. Fate presented him with as many contrasts in life as were to be found in his personality: a devoted husband and a man of strictest matrimonial morality, a warm-hearted father and an unusually kind family

man, he was married three times, one wife dying of
a chronic disease, one of the plague, and the third
betraying a nature scarcely better than that of a
harlot soon after marriage. Always hoping for a

Der Ennokrift wirt geboan in einer ftat genant grofs babilome
Vnd er würt aller vntugent vnd bofheit vol · Wenn der tüfel tüt
alles ſin vermügen dar zü Vnd das wepſt das büch/das da heiſt
Compendium Theologie·in dem ſibenden Capitel·

The birth of Antichrist
(An etching. 1475)

peaceful haven in which to live, always craving an
affluent prosperity, Agrippa was driven hither and
yon, from being the King's secretary to advocate of
the City of Metz, from city physician in Friburg to
historiographer in Lyon. He was twice arrested and
put into prison by his creditors, and enjoyed both

imperial honors and dire need and starvation. He died finally without friends, not yet fifty years old, with his dog as his only worldly possession and sole companion. The books and instruments he had loved and prized more than anything else were strewn over various parts of Germany, Switzerland, France, and the Netherlands. He died before the witch-hunting die-hards of his age had ended their voicing of calumny and hatred.

From this distance, we may look on Agrippa as the typical "restless child," the typical "failure" of the first half of the sixteenth century. He lived in an age marked by the spiritual revolt of the Reformation, by the movement of humanism, and by the destructive tightening of the ranks of reaction; his contribution to that age lies perhaps not so much in the actual originality of his writings as in the fact that he lived the cultural struggles of his time in a manner both destructive and self-destructive. The life and thought of Henry Cornelius Agrippa is an excellent summary and illustration of the sombre tragedy which the civilization of his day represented.

Even if Agrippa had none of these things to his credit, his name should be gratefully preserved in the history of medicine as that of the teacher of

107

Johann Weyer. We find Weyer as a youth of seventeen, a student under Agrippa's roof, making his first acquaintance with theoretical occultism as he turns over the pages of Trithemius' *Steganograpia* and Agrippa's writings, and with the new humanitarian protest so well represented by his teacher. And this contact in Bonn is for us of the utmost significance, for it is with the help of Agrippa that Weyer makes the greatest contribution of the Renaissance to psychological medicine.

St. Mathurin delivering the daughter of

Emperor Maximilian of a demon

(From the *Book of Hours*—XV century)

St. Mathurin delivering the daughter of
Emperor Maximilian of a demon

(From the *Life of St. Mathurin* published
in 1489.)

The devil seducing a witch
(After Ulrich Molitor's *Landis*)

LECTURE THREE

JOHANN WEYER, THE FOUNDER OF MODERN PSYCHIATRY

1

Ladies and Gentlemen:

A sorcerer riding a wolf

(After Ulrich Molitor's *Landis*)

JOHANNES WEYER was born in Grave on the Maas, Northern Brabant, in 1515 or 1516, and unlike a great many of his prominent contemporaries was a plebeian by birth. Little if anything is known of his early life; we do not even know what prompted him to take up the study of medicine. All we do know is that he studied under Cornelius Agrippa for about two years, and that when he was nineteen — approximately in 1534 — he left Agrippa's house in Bonn. While there, however, the studious Weyer had both time and opportunity to read a great many of the mysterious books which crowded the modest library of his master. Unlike Agrippa, and undoubtedly unlike many others of his day, Weyer did not come to medicine via theological or juristic studies, but wanted, first and foremost, to be a doctor. To be sure, his writings testify that he kept up an active interest not only in the general philosophical literature of his day but also in that of the ancient Greeks and Romans, and that he was a serious student of the Scriptures. Medicine, however, remained his chief interest and occupation. After the two years with Agrippa, Weyer went to Paris where he was known as Johannes Piscinarius. There, and in Orléans, he pursued his medical studies and at the age of 22 (1537) he received his medical degree from the University of Paris. As he states himself, " In Paris I made friends with a number of interesting people, mostly physicians." Obscurity enshrouds the next eight years of his life. Some biographers mistakenly assume that he travelled extensively during this time, but there is nothing to corroborate such an assumption. While Weyer refers in his writings to various customs and magic rituals observed on the island of Crete — which reference is responsible for the impression that Weyer was there — the text [1] shows clearly that Weyer is quoting Alexander of Tralles, the Byzantine physician who lived almost one thousand years before Weyer's time. However that may be, in 1545,

---

[1] Weyer, Johann, *De praestigiis daemonum,* Book IV, Ch. XVI.

at the age of thirty, Weyer was appointed city physician of Arnheim, in which capacity he served five
years. The financial resources of the town were
meagre, and when after five years the King withdrew
his part of the subsidy, it looked as if Weyer were
about to be left without means of a livelihood.
However, he was appointed personal physician to
Duke Wilhelm of Jülich-Cleve-Berg. This position
he held almost till the time of his death at the age
of seventy-two or seventy-three (he died in 1588).
The Duke was an enlightened and liberal person
who not only approved of Weyer's increasingly
liberal views but on many occasions gave him active
support.

Weyer's was a peaceful and almost unperturbed
life, devoted in its entirety to medical practice.
Judging by his first book which has since proven to
be one of the most important in the history of
medicine, Weyer must have been engaged not only
in assiduous reading while living in the ducal palace,
but also in clinical work of the most variegated kind.
It was only after some ten years of clinical research
and reading that he began to write his master work
on the prestidigitatory nature of the devil, which
was completed by 1562 and was published in 1563.

Weyer has left us a number of other smaller treatises, some of which are of more than passing interest, but we shall center our attention primarily on this, his first and most important contribution.

Although Weyer led a sedate and industrious life, one should not conclude that the man was in any way a temporizer who lacked the courage of his convictions. His was a turbulent age. The whole of Western Europe was literally aflame with the fires of the Inquisition, and Weyer was not one who could be indifferent to the suffering of others. Yet he stands out in great contrast to his master Agrippa and to Paracelsus. Agrippa's were fighting methods which the gentle and friendly warnings of his friends, even those of the highly respected Erasmus, could not moderate. Of a temperament which seemed to justify the middle name of Agrippa, given in accordance with an old Roman tradition because he was born feet first, he boasted in his correspondence, as well as in his more formal writings, of having entered life and undertaken many fights *aegris pedibus.* Weyer did not take over this mode of fighting from his teacher. Venomous abuse, so characteristic of Agrippa's style, was foreign to Weyer, as were foreign to him also the authoritarian, *ex cathedra*

112

vituperations of Paracelsus. The first of that period to investigate independently before arguing, to observe and demonstrate rather than to indulge in traditional bookish protestations, he was a singular and quite fortunate combination of keen irony such as only a Rabelais or a Montaigne could boast of, scientific steadiness, and persistent studiousness which was not equalled by any of his medical predecessors or contemporaries.

From the very outset Weyer proceeded to look upon the demoniacal world about him as an enormous clinic teeming with sick people. He set himself the task of making careful clinical studies and of using his spare time to subject to critical analysis the entire literature of his field. With unmitigated courage and sharpness of tongue, he came out frankly against the mass of ignorant monks, calling them the " encowled " and bidding them leave the management of witches and the bewitched to the physicians. Although frank and outspoken, he was neither abusive nor sacrilegious because he was a genuinely pious person. After citing a number of bishops who were opposed to the horrors of the Inquisition, he protested against the " incendiary bishops," and calmly stated that it were wiser to let ten guilty individuals go free than

VINCE
TE
IPSVM.

Plassaen Sculp.

IOANNES WIERVS.

ANNO ÆTATIS LX SALUTIS M. D. LXXVI

to put one innocent person to death, and suggested that monks would do better if they studied the art of healing instead of the art of killing. He remarked saliently, ". . . our expenses would diminish considerably if we could put to better use the logs and the bundles of fagots which are now being used to burn innocent people," and he did "not like to see how in order to destroy errors, people destroy human beings." Weyer refused to accept the "argumentation by fagots," and asked that more daylight be shed on the whole question (*luce mediana clariores*). The pain inflicted on witches he thought an unnecessary cruelty since "their illness is a sufficient pain;" he spoke of them with pity and commiseration as "*miseriae, mulierculae, dementate delusae.*" It will be recalled in this connection that the fundamental attitude of Paracelsus as regards this problem was also humanitarian, but while Paracelsus only accused and then speculated, Weyer appealed and then studied and demonstrated. The most telling illustration of his warm humanitarian feelings is Weyer's letter to his patron, the Duke, written after the manuscript of *De praestigiis daemonum* had been completed:

"Of all the misfortunes which the various fanatical and corrupt opinions, through Satan's help, have brought in our time to Christendom, not smallest is that which, under the name of witchcraft, is sown as a vicious seed. The people may be divided against themselves through their many disputes about the Scriptures and church customs while the old Snake stirs the blast, still no such great misfortune results from that as from the thereby inspired opinion that childish old hags, whom one calls witches or wizards, can do any harm to men and animals. Daily experience teaches what cursed apostasy, what friendship with the Wicked One, what hate and fighting among fellow creatures, what dissension in city and in country, what numerous murders of innocent people through the devil's wretched aid, such belief in the power of witches brings forth. No one can more correctly judge about these things than we physicians whose ears and hearts are being constantly tortured by this superstition.

"I notice more from day to day that the bog of Camarina blows its plague-laden breath stronger than ever. For a time one hoped that its poison would be gradually eliminated through the healthy teaching of the word of God; but I see that in these stormy days it reaches farther and wider than ever. In the same way, the sly devil watchfully uses each propitious circumstance. In the meantime, the pastors sleepily allow him to continue. Almost all the theologians are silent regarding this godlessness, doctors tolerate it, jurists treat it while still under the influence of old prejudices: wherever I listen, there is no one, no one who out of compassion for humanity unseals the labyrinth or extends a hand to heal the deadly wound.

"Therefore, I, with my limited means, have undertaken to dare to measure myself with this difficult affair, which disgraces our Christian Belief. It is not arrogance which impels me. I know that I know nothing, and my work allows me little free time. I know too that many others could do this work better than I. I would like to incite them to out-do me; I will gladly listen to reason.

"My object is chiefly of a theological nature: I have to set forth the artfulness of Satan according to Biblical authority and to demonstrate how one can overcome it; next, my object is philosophical, in that I fight with natural reason against the deceptions which proceed from Satan, and the crazy imagination of the so-called witches; my object is also medical, in that I have to show that those illnesses, whose origins are attributed to witches, come from natural causes; and finally, my object is legal, in that I shall have to speak of the punishment, in another than the accustomed way, of sorcerers and witches.

" But in order that I shall not meet with the reproach that I have overstepped the borders of my intellectual power and the limits of my profession with too great a faith in my own intelligence, I have submitted my seemingly paradoxical manuscript to men of Your Highness' family as well as to theologians, lawyers, and the excellent physicians, that it may be read in a critical sense. The manuscript shall remain protected through their authority if it is founded on reason; it shall fall if it is convicted of error; it shall become better if it needs supplement or revision. For there is nothing in the world which can be made immediately and at once completely perfect.

" One could rejoin here that the *Malleus Maleficarum* has already fulfilled this mission. But one has only to read in that book the silly and often godless absurdities of the theologians Heinrich Kraemer and Johann Sprenger and to compare these quietly with the contents of my manuscript. Then it will be clearly seen that I expound and advocate a totally different, even an opposite point of view.

"To you, Prince, I dedicate the fruit of my thought. For thirteen years your physician, I have heard expressed in your Court the most varied opinions concerning witches; but none so agree with my own as do yours, that witches can harm no one through the most malicious will or the ugliest exorcism, that rather their imagination — inflamed by the demons in a way not understandable to us — and the torture of melancholy makes them only fancy that they have caused all sorts of evil. For when the entire manner of action is laid on the scales, and the implements therefore examined with careful scrutiny, then soon there is shown clearly before all eyes and more lucid than the day, the nonsense and the falsity of the matter. You do not, like others, impose heavy penalties on perplexed, poor old women. You demand evidence, and only if they have actually given poison, bringing about the death of men or animals, do you allow the law to take its course.

"When a Prince of such virtues protects me, then I have faith that I can make short work of the snapping teeth of insolent quarrelers; especially since it is certain that on my side stands invincible truth. I implore God, the Highest and Best, the Father of

119

our Lord Jesus Christ, that He may profitably extend through greater employment of the Holy Spirit, what in His Benevolence He has so happily begun in Your Highness, to the honor of His Name, to the glory of Your Highness, and to the flourishing happiness of your country. Your Highness' most obedient servant, Johann Weyer, Physician."

The earnest Weyer continued somewhat later, addressing himself to the Emperor and to all worldly and ecclesiastical princes: "To all you to whom the King of Kings has entrusted the sword with which to punish the bad and to protect the good among us, I humbly submit this modest book; from the very depths of my heart and on bended knees, I pray that it will not be met with scorn as you read it and learn the views of your humblest and most respectful ward. The misdeeds of the demons whom Satan uses to shut the eyes of man and keep him in dire darkness have covered our Christian Europe with a fetid blot of shame; they have led man into the most insane error, frequent murder of innocent people, and truly severe injury of the conscience of governments. Should this manuscript meet with your disapproval, I shall at once humbly recall it, though its suppression endow me with an over-coming determination to demonstrate the truth. Should it however gain corroboration in the strength of your opinion, I shall consider myself duly rewarded for my labors. In the latter case, I would pray that people should bow to your opinion, that they should throw down their heathen views, and that the prejudices which they have absorbed through centuries be destroyed. This will come about if and when in all your countries, provinces, and estates, whenever a question of witchcraft arises, the various devilish cases be properly judged. The eye of reason will come out victorious over the misdeeds of the evil-minded; the blood of innocent people will then stop flowing so profusely, the edifice of public peace will stand firmer, the needle of conscience will sting our hearts less frequently, the rule of the devil will sink further and further away into the depths, and the Kingdom of Christ will broaden and widen its borders."

Weyer's feeling is faithfully represented in these lines. It was one of bitter skepticism concerning the general belief in witchcraft, of Christian compassion for those suffering from the cruelties of the age, and of noble aspiration to attain a new freedom and to minister to the sick. However, if Weyer had had nothing more at his disposal than his good will and social influence, he would have distinguished himself comparatively little. Fortunately, in addition to his humanitarian heart, he possessed much real medical knowledge and threw the whole weight of it into his work of denunciation. We shall see presently how he did it.

2

First of all Weyer knew what a suffering human being was; he appears to have been a very considerate, sympathetic physician who took the complaints of his patients to heart and his task of healing seriously. Utilizing his rather unusual talent of observation to the utmost, he learned to see and to describe many clinical conditions, some of which were totally new to him. He thus described what appears to have been trichinosis (at one time prevalent in the region where he lived); he gave an excellent account of the English sweating sickness and of syphilis; he described "pestilencial cough" (apparently influenza and influenza pneumonia), and erysipelas; and, according to Sprengel, he left us a remarkable study of scurvy. In every case, Weyer refused to base his judgment on hearsay, but went himself directly to the bedside to verify clinical facts. As we have seen,

122

various and odd foreign bodies were supposed to be deposited in human organisms by the devil. Weyer did not deny this merely out of skepticism but, in a manner quite different from that of Lange, he personally investigated such cases. At one time he visited a sixteen-year-old girl from whose mouth he extracted a heavy wad of cloth and several other objects. The father stated that the girl frequently vomited up objects which he was certain the devil had introduced into her stomach. Weyer proceeded to palpate the girl's abdomen and found that one could not get any tactile perception of a foreign body lodged in the stomach. Then he inquired as to the girl's meal hours, and pointed out the fact that no signs of chylus nor of any other food particles were visible on the piece of cloth, although it had supposedly come from the stomach and the girl had had her regular meal only a short time before. The examination finished, Weyer went carefully into the history of the girl's trouble and traced it to a stomach-ache which she had tried to cure by drinking some sort of water bought at a cross-road because it was presented to her as Holy Water. Evidently it was a case of mild hysterical malingering; yet the patient was supposed to feel better when a sign of

123

the Cross was made over her. Weyer remarks in this instance that while he is naturally not at all disrespectful of the Cross, he mentions this case in order to show how misused it is at times, and concludes: " These are the consequences which must be suffered when one turns away from the natural remedies given to us by the Lord and through Him created by man to things which only nourish the unjustified insanity of witchcraft."

Weyer submitted such phenomena as pseudocyesis to the same type of careful investigation. He studied various atresias in the newborn, and like a worthy younger contemporary of Vesalius did not join with the tradition ascribing such anomalies to human degeneracy or to the assumed fact that such newborn are conceived by witches through incubi, but investigated each case and came to see the natural phenomenon in its proper light. He observed some examples of atresias of the *os uteri* and of unusually hyperplastic hymens. When the phenomenon of suppression of the menstrual flow came to his attention he proceeded to make a careful examination; he described in detail, and in an almost modern manner, what the posture of the patient should be while under such examination, how to proceed and how to expose the field of observation to the best advantage. Not a surgeon himself, he tells us how, at least on two occasions, he sought the help of a surgeon who was apparently more than a little frightened, but who nevertheless did the bidding of the personal physician to the Duke and, using a razor, cut open the hymen to release the mass of accumulated blood and henceforth reestablish the normal menstrual flow. Weyer was one of the first to use paracentesis in ascites. He pursued all these studies as a clinician and not as a medical literary student only. As a matter of fact, it is difficult if not impossible to find a medical book written before Weyer's time that contains as many expressions of the "I saw," "I observed," "Doctor So-and-so reports," "I knew a man" nature as fill Weyer's works, for Weyer seems to have based all his arguments and all his conclusions on little else than clinical material. Speculation, particularly pure speculation, seems to have been foreign to his positivistic medical thinking. When he heard of a young girl whose fasting had become a notorious case — such phenomena were frequently reported in those days — Weyer looked up the girl (her name was Barbara and she came from the town of Unn), took her with her sister into

125

his own house and proceeded to study the case. It did not take him long to discover that Barbara was a malingerer, in spite of a certificate from the Senate of Unn testifying to her being supernatural, and that her appetite was anything but pathological. She was fed secretly by her sister Eliza, whom Weyer jestingly dubbed her "Habakkuk." This serenely observational and lucidly experimental method was more than unique at the turn of the first half of the sixteenth century, and alone would justify the characterization of Weyer by Albrecht von Haller: "He was a man whose spirit tore itself out beyond the confines of his age and who actively and forcefully exposed the true nature of witches and the possessed."

The quietness and lucidity of Weyer's temperament cannot be over-emphasized; it not only served him personally in good stead, but in his day and age it was a unique characteristic that deserves particular attention. It was a century of panic, suspicion, and sadistic excesses that only an insane rage could create. Here and there one saw or heard of a man with real sympathetic warmth in his heart, but such spirits as the poet Hans Sachs (1494-1576), the older contemporary of Johann Weyer, were few and far between. Certainly the manner in which the social

126

" motive " of his day is reflected in Sachs' poems was the exception rather than the rule, particularly in the medical profession. Sachs was responsible for such things as:

" Des Teuffels eh und reutterey
Ist nur gespenst und fantasey
Das bockfaren kumpt auss missglauben.

. . .

Diss als ist haidnisch und ein spot
Bey den, die nicht glauben in Got.
So du im glauben Gott erkenst,
So kann dir schaden kein gespenst."

The same good humor that we see here in Sachs is also to be found in Weyer who, citing the Roman satirical poet A. Persius Flaccus, exclaimed, " *O curas hominum o quantum est in rebus inane!* " (Oh, cares of man, how inane some of them are!)

But Europe as a whole was raving mad — some years after the appearance of his chief work Weyer issued a special treatise covering over one hundred and eighty pages on the disease of wrath.[2] He stated that as a physician he remained within his professional

---

[2] *Wieri, J., De irae morbo, ejusdem curatione philosophica, medica et theologica liber, Basiliae 1577.*

province in attacking this mass phenomenon because he considered it a serious disease requiring not only philosophic and theologic, but also medical treatment. The picture Weyer painted was of necessity morbid, but as a real scientist and physician he could not shirk the painful duty of faithfully and accurately describing the horrible, or of citing endless examples of human cruelty; of recalling, for instance, how Pope Stephen VI unearthed the body of the Antipope Formosus and cut off the fingers, throwing them into the river to be eaten by the fishes; or of relating in detail the individual horrors of the Inquisition and the cruelties of the wars of his day. He gave religious, philosophical, and detailed medical advice on how to be cured of this madness, then epidemic, and concluded with the words: "Why don't we follow, rather, the examples of humility and kindness which history offers us? Philipp of Macedonia, his son Alexander, Julius Caesar, Titus — all these put us Christians to shame. The Sultan Saladin showed great humanness in relation to the prisoners of the Crusades who happened to fall into his hands: he gave them gifts and sent them into Christian countries; he had respect for their courageous resistance; when Jerusalem was stormed, he gave gifts to the crying widows of the

128

fallen and released them to go to their respective homes. If only you Christian cities could teach the kindness of a barbarian, thou City of Zütphen, City of Naarden, City of Haarlem!"

That Weyer was closely in touch with the trends and drives of his age, that his point of view was highly "socialized," is clear. How much more striking, in the light of this sensitiveness and responsiveness, is the unquestionable poise and extreme evenness of spirit he displays when, as a true scientist, he discusses the most burning problems of his day. In thought and in fact, Weyer followed in the footsteps of Seneca. Seneca wrote his *De ira* when he was Nero's preceptor, and like Weyer and his *De praestigiis* he wrote it for the benefit of an emotionally disorganized generation. Hence Weyer reminded his readers of Seneca's *Multos absolvemus si caeperimus ante judicare quam irasci.*[3]

Let us turn to the pages of Weyer's chief work, whose power, method, and tenor we are now better prepared to understand and correctly interpret.

[3] Seneca, *De ira.* 3, XXIX.

3

The title page of Weyer's chief work reads as follows: *De praestigiis daemonum, et incantationibus, ac veneficiis, Libri V. Authore Joanne Wiero medico. Cum Caesareae Maijest. gratia et privilegio. Basileae, per Joannem Oporinum. 1563.*

The title itself already contains a hint as to Weyer's trend of thought. It suggests that the author intends to look into the matter with an eye to the illusions created by demons rather than to the wickedness performed by those supposedly allied with the devil; it definitely suggests that the author wants to view the subject as a medical man should; and by the use of the word *veneficis* instead of the word *maleficis*, it at once conveys the thought that a more rational approach to witchcraft than a mere recital of the esoteric performances of evil by alleged sorcerers may be sought. As a matter of fact, Weyer does attempt — and quite successfully — to demonstrate that a number of injuries inflicted or suffered by witches were due to the action of certain drugs or poisons, and so uses the word *veneficis* with specific meaning. Throughout the book Weyer repeatedly declares to the reader, and most particularly to his adversaries, his right as a physician to delve

into the refinements of the law covering the treatment of witches "because truth may be sought
wherever it can be found." Time and again he calls
to mind that although a member of the medical profession he retains the right to look into theology and
the Scriptures for his facts and arguments, because
"these domains should not be considered outside
the scope of a medical man's work." Was not Saint
Luke a physician in Antioch before becoming one of
the Evangelists? In short, we see Weyer through the
pages of his book not as a narrow-minded specialist
or dogmatic exponent of his views, but rather as an
enlightened man who, meeting the insane masters
of the age on their own ground, defeats them with
their own weapons. Although extremely pious,
Weyer remains reasonable and rationalistic, scourg-
ing the witch-hunters and their servants in a manner
both frank and unreserved yet without blasphemy.
He reminds the Inquisitors of Isaiah's denunciatory
words: "They also have erred through wine, and
through strong drink are out of the way: the priest
and the prophet have erred through strong drink,
they are swallowed up of wine, they are out of the
way through strong drink; they err in vision, they

stumble *in* judgment." [4] Again using the words of
the same prophet he reminds the judges, torturers,
and executioners of his day: "We have made a
covenant with death, and with hell are we at agreement; when the overflowing scourge shall pass
through, it shall not come unto us: for we have
made lies our refuge, and under falsehood have we
hid ourselves." [5]

Weyer's own words could serve as a motto for the
entire treatise: "Love your fellow beings, destroy
errors, fight for the truth without any cruelty; (and
remember the Apostle who said) let those exercise
against us their cruelty who do not know with what
pain truth is obtained and with what great difficulties
one guards one's self against errors (Book VI)."
It would be a mistake, however, to assume that
Weyer is merely a sentimental, liberal-minded court
physician; on the contrary, he is strictly matter of
fact and rationalistic. In the first book of the
treatise he definitely states that the devil knows
nothing about human thought and he refuses to accept the popular belief that the devil can enter into
a contract with a human being; in another connection

[4] *The Holy Bible*, Isaiah 28: 7.
[5] *Ibid.*, 28: 15.

he even goes so far as to state that contrary to wide-
spread belief the devil is not even afraid of the sign
of the Cross — why should he be, since he was not
afraid to face Christ himself? Weyer then proceeds
to analyze all those passages in the Scriptures on
which the capital punishment of witches was supposed to have been based. The traditional references
quoted by the masters of the witch-hunting epidemic,
such as Exodus 18 and 20, or Leviticus 19, 20, 27,
and 31, were according to Weyer grossly misunderstood; he studied Latin, Greek, and Hebrew texts
and came to the conclusion that the Hebrew word
khasaph meant not wizardry and magic of a supernatural type but the art of mixing various injurious
substances and he even demonstrated the action of
various drugs involved in so-called witchcraft. We
shall return to this subject when we consider Weyer's
clinical observations at closer range.

From the outset Weyer denounces superstition as
heathenism and subjects all those physicians, quacks,
and wizards who resort to exorcism, magic, and other
non-medical methods to scathing attack: "And this
is how these good pillars of the Church stand out as
the principal slaves of Beelzebub; the latter should
glory in the fact that he is well served, chiefly by

those who act under the mantle of religion; for in order to collect more money and as if to divert themselves from the monotony of being held in great esteem, they sell their souls and those of others and devote them to various devils." They overlook natural diseases of man and cause injury to human lives — all to the detriment of "medicine which is the most ancient, the most useful, and the most necessary of all the sciences (Book VI)." As to the members of the medical profession, only "ignorant physicians refer a man bitten by a mad dog or afflicted with epilepsy to the Saints of the Church" and "the uneducated physicians and surgeons cover their own stupidity and mistakes by the use of sorcery and by virtue of the Saints (Book II)."

While expressing these criticisms, Weyer more than once recalls his teacher Cornelius Agrippa and in his usual terse language tries to explode some of the fantastic tales which have been circulated about his first master. Speaking of Agrippa's dog, he says: "I cannot stop wondering how people of high esteem can talk and write such unadulterated foolishness, unless it be just mean and empty blabber. I knew that black dog very well while I was in Bonn. It was a dog of moderate size and his name was *Monsieur*; quite frequently when Agrippa was out walking, I would accompany him leading the dog on a rope. It was a common, human dog and his master provided him with a companion, a bitch of the same color and stature; he acquired her while I was there and gave her the name of *Mademoiselle*. As I see it, the cause for all this insane gossip [6] was Agrippa's almost childish love for that dog, which is quite

[6] Cf. Lecture Two. This superstitious gossip about Agrippa's dog was kept alive from decade to decade and from century to century. Though few, if any, had read Agrippa's writings, scarcely anyone was ignorant of the foolish story which was accepted as pure fact and was known all over Europe and England. It is an interesting reflection on the psychology of Europe, a psychology that held its sway for centuries. Samuel Butler, who died almost one hundred and fifty years after Agrippa, wrote in his *Hudibras:*

> " Agrippa kept a Stygian pug
> I'the garb and habit of a dog
> That was his tutor and the cur
> Read to th'occult philosopher,
> And taught him subtly to maintain
> All other sciences are vain."

and Robert Southey, who died almost three hundred years after Agrippa (1843) was still echoing reverberations of the ghostlike memory when he wrote of some of the manuscripts in Agrippa's library:
> " The letters were written with blood therein
> And the leaves were made of dead man's skin."

This was the psychological air in which Weyer was born, lived, and died. Cf. also for many characteristic details: Morley, Henry, *The Life of Cornelius Agrippa*, 2 vols. (London, 1856).

usual with some people. On occasion, he would kiss him; he would let him sit at the table at my side and allow him to sleep in his bed. The dog would always roam about our study room and would rest among highly valuable manuscripts and on our common study table. It is also possible that the talk was caused by the fact that though my host sat most of the time in his warm house and went out but once a week, he always knew what was going on in the world; even when I lived there some foolish people ascribed this to the fact that the dog was the devil; in reality the situation was as follows: Agrippa received daily letters from various countries written by the most learned men of the time (Book II)."

To him the story of the witch of Endor was incorrect; she had *not* raised Samuel from his tomb. He had little respect for the monks, priests, and quacks who dealt with the problem of witchcraft. "They are mostly quite uneducated and therefore entirely shameless people (the good and pious among them whom I respect are excluded). They claim that they know a little medicine and they lie to the person who seeks help when they say that his illness is due to bewitchment. Not satisfied with this alone, they brand forever some innocent matron and her whole family with the mark of *witch*; they smother the innocent with their hatred, they break up friendships, separate blood relations, and manage horrors of the dungeons. This fate befalls not only poor innocent people but also the one who dares to take up the defence of these victims (Book II)."

Weyer exclaims: "The story of the manner in which the witch gives herself to the devil is unreasonable and untrue. The *Witch's Hammer* relates two methods. The first is the solemn gathering of all the witches in the presence of Satan; the other a private meeting (of the future witch) with Satan in some place. They (the witches) promise then to deny their faith, not to accept the Holy Sacrament, and to stamp upon the Crucifix with their feet. They are supposed to eat children, or cook them and prepare various salves out of their bones, which when rubbed into their skins make possible their flights through the air. . . . That all this nonsense does not deserve any credence is clear. This alliance comes about merely through the fact that the devil poisons human fantasies so that the individual sees all sorts of visions and hears all sorts of voices. There is, however, no question of a real contract to which one of the parties forces the other by means of deception." Weyer's reference here to the devil as the originator of auditory and optic hallucination could be easily misunderstood — actually it has been by many readers. It is doubtful whether Weyer believed in the existence of the devil at all, for it is hardly an exaggeration to say that the word *devil* in the sixteenth century covered the same multitude of sins as do today the words *complex* or *inferiority complex* which have crept into common usage without, however, conveying any definite scientific concept. As one reads the text of *De praestigiis daemonum*, one obtains a clear impression that Weyer uses the word *devil* in rather a free manner and somewhat as we use the colloquial expression *crazy*. At no time, despite frequent references to the devil, does Weyer depart from the positivistic, empirical, and medical point of view. He himself summarizes this attitude quite clearly in the Fifth Book of the treatise when he says: "We ought to resort now to other means than those which heretofore have been held by custom as unassailable. And these means will conform much more with the doctrine of Jesus Christ and His Apostles when we want to be rid of Satan and cure ourselves of his sorcery. First of all, and before anything else is done, as soon

138

as one observes some ailment which is engendered against the order of nature, one has to resort, in accordance with the ordinance of the Lord, to him who is known through doctrine, profession, and usage as one who well understands various maladies, their differences, their signs, their causes, that is to say, to a physician in good standing."

Thus Weyer, having carefully reviewed all theological and philosophical arguments, turns towards clinical demonstrations and pathological physiology. He never asks the reader to believe him on the basis of his authority alone. When he wants to prove a point he always emphasizes that he will do so by examination of the clinical fact. For instance — and this is typical of all his arguments — in order to prove the pathological hallucinatory nature of some of the stories related by witches, Weyer states: " Thus, in order that this thing, in itself obscure and covered with darkness, be clarified by examples, I shall presently relate the confessions of two women who were recently taken and burned in one of our imperial cities; these two confessions were taken by me from the judiciary registery with the consent of the Consul and I shall add to these a third one (Book VI)." This is but a sample of Weyer's method which we shall follow in more detail somewhat later. For the present, let us turn to what Weyer has to say about those members of his own profession who are the too-believing children of their own age.

We recall that chronicity was, according to the *Malleus Maleficarum,* one of the differential points in favor of a diagnosis of sorcery; Weyer answers this with: " The uninformed and the unskilful physicians relegate all the incurable diseases, or all the diseases the remedy for which they overlook, to witchcraft. When they do this, they are talking about disease like a blind man does about color. Like many surgeons with their quackery, they cover their ignorance of our Sacred Art with the playthings of magic male-factors and they themselves are thus the real male-factors. To these also belong the windbags of the school of Theophrastus Paracelsus. Aping their master they promise golden mountains. . . . They stamp with their feet on old medical science and yet they accomplish nothing. That proud man consid-ered himself the monarch and the discoverer of the real medicine. I should not want, however, my objections to be construed to mean that I am opposed to chemistry. Exactly the contrary is true. I am pleased to the depth of my heart and I congratulate our Art on the fact that chemistry is at present so assiduously studied and applied. Thanks to chemistry, we are able to obtain various distillates, oils, powders, and salts out of minerals and metals which can be used against a number of afflictions. This I readily admit; I myself set store in these substances for I use them not without success (Book II)." To Weyer, then, all priests and monks who resort to exorcisms and similar methods are " abusers of the name of the Lord " and " ecclesiastic magicians." His conscience and principles set forth, Weyer proceeds with his clinical investigations.

4

Weyer minces no words in expounding his conviction that the devil is devoid of power — that evil spirits cannot transform blood into water, or dust into lice, or sweet into salty water (Book I) — and he seeks first of all to separate one definite group of clinical occurrences from the apparently amorphous mass that was the psychopathology and the mystical medicine of his day. That he tried to prove that the Hebrew word for wizard and witch had originally meant poison-maker or poison-mixer has already

141

been mentioned. He further states: "The Germans designate by one word *Zauberer* both the imposter-magician who makes impostures his business, and the witch who is deceived by the devil because of the stupidity of her spirit and the corruption of her fantasy; they also give the same name to the poison-maker (Book II)." Weyer, true to his clinical sense, does not limit himself to a mere declaration of his convictions but with his skeptical, active rationalism seeks for empirical corroboration of his hypothesis. "It is a devilish fantasy — the assertion of witches that they kill newborn babies by means of certain ceremonies; the same can be said concerning the statement that they exhume the bodies of these children from their graves and use them to prepare certain salves. All this is so terrifying that if I myself had experienced and seen it, I could only say that my imagination had deceived me. But let us assume that all this is true, the question then arises where-from does such a salve get its power? For according to the *Witch's Hammer,* if one covers one's self with such a salve or even sits down on a chair that is covered with such a salve, one rises into and is transported through the air (Book III)." Weyer investigates the various salves and other remedies or drugs that are used in the form of herbs, lotions, and powders and comes to rather revealing conclusions. He relates that his friend Dr. Johann Echt of Cologne communicated to him a case of mysterious hematuria which was traced to the use of cantharides; he tells of his own case of Frau Anna von Virmont whom he personally treated in 1554 and whose affliction he traced to the arsenic which her fifteen-year-old chamber maid secretly administered to her. Weyer's procedure in this case is reminiscent of our best contemporary heroic experimenters in modern medicine — to verify and prove his diagnosis he himself tasted the soup which he suspected of containing arsenic. The various somnolent and stupor-like states of the alleged witches he ascribes to the effect of certain deadening drugs described at some length in Book II. But before speaking in more detail of Weyer's interest in drugs, I should like to cite a brief report by him that is both characteristic of the background of the age and of his trend of thought.

Weyer saw an interesting case of " an executioner of Antwerp, a Frenchman, who despite the fact that he had committed a thousand evil deeds known to everyone, could not be forced to confess the truth no matter to what cruel tortures he was subjugated. For no sooner had the torture begun than he would sink into a state of alienation and loss of all his senses. The very wise Senate of the city made inquiries from ordinary physicians who stated that such a stupor could not be produced by anything other than soporific medicaments such as we described in chapter seventeen of our Book II of this treatise. I may also add that the Lord permitted that he should endure the torture . . . and having been tortured in various manners he was executed without showing any signs of repentance because he was so stuporous and drunk with the blood of an infinite number of people whom he had done to death (Book V)."

To return now to Weyer's pharmacological investigations: We next find Weyer studying the actions of atropin "which the Italian people call Belladonna" and *cannabis indica* which appears in the treatise under the oriental name of *hieran-luc,* of Thebaic opium and hyocyamus. It is to the action of these and similar drugs that he ascribes many of the weird psychological experiences of the witches. He warns against believing literally in the various statements made by witches because, he says, these are

144

but expressions of delirious fantasies in which the witches themselves believe as realities. He describes what is well-known to us as the atropin jag — the state of excitement, the state of tremulous anxiety, the optic hallucinations which are reminiscent of our present day *delirium tremens*. He explains the many sexual fantasies of witches by the fact that they rub the various salves into their skins and mucous membranes of the genital organs, thus absorbing the poison into their systems. " They frequently abuse of the natural remedies which are given to them for their comfort." Weyer gives the formula of one such salve and remarks, apparently in regard to *hieran- luc,* " they think they see theatres, beautiful gardens, feasts, beautiful ornaments, clothes, handsome young men, kings, magistrates, in short, all those things which delight them and which they thus believe themselves to be enjoying; they also see devils, ravens, prisons, deserts, and other torments. These are therefore the causes of violent dreams (Book III)."

It is as interesting as it is significant that all the descriptions given by Weyer concern themselves with the ideational content of the afflicted, a point the importance of which was not properly appreciated by clinical psychiatry until the very close of the nineteenth century. By means of the study of this ideational content Weyer attempts to explain specifically many of the hallucinatory experiences which the Inquisitors and the lay judges accepted as realities. The case of an Italian is quoted, who before attending the Witches' Sabbath would treat himself with a medicamentous suppository, apparently containing belladona. And " should these unfortunates happen to wander into the path of those other erring people, then frequently their lot is death; and even if the injurious power of the poison works insidiously they find their death (as witches) long before it finally strikes the heart, which is the source of all life."

Weyer makes a brief excursion into veterinary medicine and after proper investigation absolves the witch from the wide-spread suspicion that she was the cause of epidemics among cattle and beasts of burden. Instead of condemning the witch to death, Weyer advises fumigation with sulphur and aromatic substances, a modern and quite effective remedy, as a cure for the epidemic.

Never failing to keep his chief thesis uppermost in mind, never deviating from the path of medical endeavor, Weyer again and again repeats his refrain: " In all such cases a good doctor is to be consulted because nothing is more important than to make the clinical situation as clear as daylight, for in no domain of human life are human passions so freely at play as in this one, these passions being superstition, rage, hate, and malice (Book VI)." [7]

5

One by one Weyer undermines the pseudo-anatomical and pseudo-physiological props which supported the current beliefs exposed in the *Malleus Maleficarum*. It was three quarters of a century since Sprenger and Kraemer had published their *Malleus* when Weyer completed his *De praestigiis daemonum*, yet little actual change had taken place since the days when the two friar preachers had exacted the approbation for their book from the University of Cologne. A trick of a circus juggler was still considered a weird miracle performed by Satan and was still punishable by death; sexual impotence was still considered a bewitchment, a sin, a crime, or all three together; and werewolves were still regarded

[7] Cf. also Binz, Carl, *op. cit.*, pp. 57-58.

as realities. Weyer's was the task of confuting these
superstitions which appeared to have become chronic.
We find him therefore observing even jugglers and
tight-rope performers in order to establish the true
nature of the phenomenon, as it were. " Simple
folk consider certain things miraculous which, although marvelous from a certain point of view, can
be witnessed every day and proven to be performed
by the agile, simple hands of various tricksters. Pom-
ponatius,[8] in his book on enchantments, tells us that
he saw in Mantua and Padua one of the masters of
this business, Reatio by name, perform marvelous
tricks and that the man was therefore thought to have
dealings with evil spirits, arrested by the Inquisition,
and tortured. But he revealed to the Inquisitors the
secrets of his trade, demonstrating to them that it
was all based on imposture and agility of hands and
that he always played his game with the aid of other
individuals who knew the tricks of deception. He
was released, only to be later murdered by someone on the road (Book I)." Through such factual
approach Weyer seeks not only to undermine the
authority of the devil but to prepare a sufficient

[8] Pietro Pomponazzi, a liberal teacher in the University of Padua
towards the end of the fifteenth century.

foundation for a rational physiological psychology and psychopathology.

He takes up the problem of impotence which apparently was a question of some magnitude in those days since the *Malleus* discusses the subject repeatedly and in much detail, and since traditional medicine rarely deviated in this respect from the views of Sprenger and Kraemer. Weyer refuses to see in impotence anything but a natural result of physiological causes. He mocks at the popular remedial measures which were used in those days: "They write various letters on fresh parchment to which they ascribe a great significance and they consider this the supreme secret remedy against such trouble. They murmur a Psalm of David seven times over this piece of parchment and then they tie it to the groin of the afflicted husband — well, I shall not tell more about it. I should like only to state that such a prescription must have been made up in hell (Book V)." And in another instance: "Nicholas and William Varignana, Doctors of Medicine, and Peter Argellat, Surgeon, say the bewitched husband who is unable to live with his wife should urinate through the wedding ring." Weyer refuses to consider these accepted practises seriously. With his characteristic sense of humor he says: "Reader, I shall tell you a secret, I shall teach you another very ridiculous mode of treatment which is nevertheless practiced faithfully by a lady whose name is Katherine Loe and whose children I know personally. Having noticed that her husband seemed to have lost the virtue of manhood, and having tried various methods to cure him of his trouble, she went to the Cathedral in Everfield, which is in the Duchy of Mont, and presented herself at the altar of Saint Anthony. Then she took a piece of wax in the form of a viril member and devotedly hung it up on the altar, hoping by this means to restore the strength of her husband. The curé, who knew nothing of this offering, came to the altar with his eyes lowered and almost closed, said the canons of the Mass, and then, as is the custom, he opened his eyes and lifted them upward. There was the woman's offering. Suddenly recognizing what it was, he exclaimed in loud anger: ' Remove that devil from there! ' " This somewhat Rabelaisian story is characteristic of Weyer in more than one respect; it is of particular interest to us because it demonstrates how this very pious man, discreet of thought and tongue, discards all bigotry when he wants to drive home a fact.

However, the closer Weyer approaches the problem of the more salient mental diseases the more serious grows his mood. At times the chapter-heading alone represents a clear statement of his belief. Thus the heading of chapter twenty-three, Book IV, reads: " Of the malady called lycanthropy in which human beings believe themselves to have been transformed into wolves and who are popularly called werewolves." In Book III he states that if one occasionally encounters dangerous wolves who run about wildly and who are thought to be witches, known in the German language as *vveuuoffs*, " one should consider them real wolves." As to those who believe themselves to be wolves, " they are tormented and pushed by the devil (which to Weyer means that they are mentally sick. — G. Z.) into all sorts of tragedy." These people speak of their wanderings as werewolves or lycanthrops because this " fantasy fills their organs" and because " their imagination is corrupted," that is, pathologically disturbed. " I knew a melancholic who insisted that he smelled sulphur and tar and that whatever was offered him to eat tasted of pepper, and yet it could easily be seen that all this was not true. He also stated that his sexual organs were terribly painful with inflamation and evil smells and he feared lest they become foul, and yet these organs were quite normal. I could cite here an infinite number of examples so that you would easily see . . . how one single humor, or the fuming vapors of black bile, affect the seat of the mind and produce all such monstrous fantasies (Book III)."

Such disturbances of the human imagination seem to fascinate the clinical curiosity of Weyer, but no matter how great his scientific detachment, his argument is almost always punctuated with severe criticism of, and reproach against, the tradition of his day. Pondering these phenomena, Weyer apparently accepts customary belief when he says that the devil might sneak into a human body and cause disease. Job was thus injured, Nebuchadnezzar ate grass like a beast, and individuals possessed by evil spirits flocked to be treated by Christ. "It is fortunate," he adds, "that they (Job, Nebuchadnezzar) are not among us today, for if they were hereabouts some old woman would have to shoulder the responsibility for their distress, and the brains of these old women are so inflamed that under torture they would confess to having caused all these terrors."

"A malicious complaint and insane suspicion on the

part of the vulgar and stupid populace compel our judges to catch some poor old woman whose mind the devil made insane and throw her into holes which are more like robber caves than prisons; once there, they are turned over to henchmen for cruel torture and, while thus tormented with unutterable pain, they are questioned. Guilty or innocent — it does not matter! They are not relieved until they confess. And so it comes to pass that they prefer to surrender their souls to the Lord through flames than to suffer longer under the torture of these horrible tyrants. Should they die under the very fists of the henchman, smothered by their cruelty, or should they expire at the time when, reduced to skeletons, they are taken out of their incarceration, then the Powers that Be write jubilantly that these poor creatures have committed suicide (which they might very well have done as a result of the torture or the filth of the dungeon) or they say that the devil broke their necks." Weyer expresses hope in the second coming of Christ — he hopes that some day the " Judge of All Things " will do justice to all the " pitiless judges " of his day. " Strange things," he exclaims, " come at times from the human mouth." This might well be understood in both the

direct and the figurative sense. Weyer then reports
the case of the girl (of whom we spoke at the beginning of this lecture) who was supposed to vomit
pieces of cloth, and further stresses the importance of understanding that human imagination may
lead man astray and into a number of mental aberra-
tions. As for Weyer's literary style, which can be
seen here to good advantage, whole pages of *De praestigiis daemonum* seem to have been inspired with
the same fire and justifiable rancor that is so characteristic of Friedrich of Spee who continued the
battle about fifty years after Weyer's death —
almost three-quarters of a century after Weyer had
begun the fight. However, Weyer's humanistic
fervor, great as it was, was not his foremost contribution. We cannot stress too much or too frequently that Weyer never lost sight of his clinical
empiricism, and that he was the real inaugurator
of scientific method in relation to medical psychology.

To return to the problem: Weyer appeals to the
reason of the reader when he says that many of those
women regarded as witches preferred death to the
tragedy which their lives had become. " They will
confess to any kind of shameful act about which
they are questioned in order to make certain that

they will not be returned to the terrible holes in which they are kept. Recently a poor old woman was compelled to confess that during the previous year, in 1565, she had produced terrific rainstorms, caused an unusually cold winter, and kept the ground frozen far into the Spring. And yet there were enough serious men who believed firmly and implicitly in all this, although it is impossible to fathom anything more stupid in this world. This was recently reported to me in writing by the distinguished and venerable Abbot of Echternach, Doctor Antonius Hovaeus (Book IV)." Weyer continues in his effort to undermine the superstitious credulity of people when speaking of the foolish belief that the devil though unseen, can put into human beings various objects such as large nails or long needles. ". . . of course these objects could not come up from below, even if the oesophagus were stretched to the utmost. In Nimwegen there was a man who at Easter attempted to swallow a whole egg, but he choked to death." Weyer devotes the whole of Book IV to this problem of foreign bodies.

However, aside from the weird confessions made under torture, what are the various tales told by numberless strange women? The heading of Book

III is a partial answer to this question: " The witches do not produce the diseases to which they confess to be the cause. And it is to be proven here that all that is told concerning them does not deserve to be considered as anything else than pure fable."

" Let us therefore speak now of that terrible state called nightmare, and look carefully and fully into what truth there is in it in order that the fantasy of false beliefs be removed forever, not only from the minds of the people, but also from the heads of some learned men (Book III)." Weyer recalls Pliny, Avicenna, Averroes, and Themison who gave their own names to this state, such as *albealion* or *alcranum* (Avicenna) or *puigalia* (Themison). Due to certain pathological imprints on the animal spirits, individuals experience feelings (we would say today hallucinatory states) now joyous, boisterous, and merry, and then sad, quiet, and morose, during which they " endure all sorts of unpleasant things now human, then bestial, now oppressive and stifling, then airy or floating," and through these experiences " the senses are so affected and impressed that it seems as if all these things were actually occurring. As a result of this, it so happens that a man might think that he is an ass with a bag on his back, or that he is a flying eagle; at times such people might think that they are flying with Diana and her Nymphs, or that they are transported from plain to plain with a host of other women dancing, travelling in far-off lands, or attending various follies. Such things occur mostly at night and not so frequently during the day, except for those demented melancholics who persist in experiencing while awake the same things as normal people do in their sleep. Varron, according to Nonnius, calls all these images somnorines, that is to say ghosts of sleep (Book III)." One can hardly over-estimate the importance and the depth of this statement which seems now to us only obvious and self-understood. Its significance will become clear if we recall that not until the first quarter of the twentieth century was it clinically discovered that there is no essential difference between the delusionary and hallucinatory trends of our schizophrenias or the delirious experiences of some of the toxemias and the dreams of normal individuals. Moreover, the very attempt to approximate the normal and the pathological psychologies of man and to consider them similar in content puts Weyer so far ahead of his and succeeding centuries that the words of Albrecht von Haller become doubly justified.

157

From the various quotations cited, it has perhaps been noticed that Weyer carefully kept before his mental eye the detailed text of the *Malleus Maleficarum*. This is evident in his consideration of the various drugs, of impotence, and of lycanthropy; in his treatment of the somnorines — when he disposes of the problem of transvection, and of sexual congress with the devil — when he answers the *Malleus* with "What they call incubus is nothing but a state which is popularly called *mar*." In this connection it is interesting to note that Weyer takes the word *incubus*, popularly designating an evil spirit of specific sexual propensities, and boldly calls it a state of mind. "This (state of mind) comes from the fact that vapors of phlegm and of black bile rise into the brain. The individual under these conditions imagines that something heavy sprawls over his body. This usually occurs when the person lies on his back and when the stomach is filled with heavy, sticky mucous or is loaded with food. That is why melancholic women when they lie asleep on their backs . . . imagine and then state that an unclean spirit came and violated them. Recently I myself observed a similar case; a priest came to consult me because a woman with whom he was well-acquainted would come to him nightly in the form of an oppressive and tormenting incubus (succubus). He sought advice of a monk and an old woman, but obtained no relief. After a certain time I succeeded in explaining to him the nature of his illness and was able to discharge him, the prognosis pointing to improvement (Book III)." Seeking for a more rational and positivistic approach, Weyer states that he who is not inclined to be slow-witted can easily see the absurdities of current beliefs which do not deserve to be given credence, for there are individuals who through the complexion of their temperaments are more prone to be attacked by these follies; "they are melancholics who when suffering a minor loss, or for some other reason, fall very easily into a state of sadness (Book III)." It is all a matter of the proper balance of one's imagination.

Weyer, like his younger contemporary Vives, but using clinical facts to support his contention (Vives was not a physician), stresses the importance of affects in the pathogenesis of mental disease. Of all affects, he considers love and fear the most powerful in their effect on imagination. "Imagination," says Weyer, "represents the activity of reason under the influence of objects that affect our senses; imagination is capable of setting one's fantasies outward, and reaching much further than the activity of our senses, it transgresses them because it feigns the presence of images without the senses being directly stimulated; in brief, imagination is protean in its capacity, it is like a cameleon (Book III)." While this formulation still bears many characteristics of the traditional psychology of *virtutes*, the thought contained therein is as advanced as it is significant. Weyer not only attempts here to describe the whole process of the formation of delusions and hallucinations, but also to bring some unity into the whole problem by conceiving the process as a series of gradations in the relationship between sensation received from external stimuli and their intrapsychic representations. Under particularly severe circumstances these become independent generators of pathological images such as delusions and hallucinations. Evidently this view — today old and almost trite — marks not only a serious advance over Weyer's medical predecessors, but presents a still more important implication to which we shall return towards the latter part of the lecture.

It is obvious that this trend in medical psychology, if it was to be utilized at all clinically, required a careful and understanding study of the patient's ideational content. The clinical value of this study — in which Weyer was a most effective pioneer — even Kraepelin was inclined to question towards the very close of the nineteenth century. It was first most successfully developed and utilized by American psychiatry as late as the beginning of our century under the influence of the newer trends of dynamic psychology (Adolph Meyer, August Hoch, George H. Kirby, and their more consistent pupils). Sensing more than understanding the importance of the ideational content, Weyer seldom fails to give a graphic picture of the mentally sick individual. He describes one such case: " I knew a melancholic Italian who thought he was Emperor and Monarch of the whole world, and who insisted that he was the only one who had a right to these titles; in all other respects he remained clear in his speech, was quite at ease and suffered from no other illness. Yet he took a singular delight in composing Italian rhymes dealing with the state of Christianity, the various effects of religion, and the methods of appeasing the unrest in France and in Flanders, as if all these things had been revealed to him from Heaven; on each and every occasion he marked his titles with the following letters: R. R. D. D. M. M., that is, *Rex Regum, Dominus Dominantium, Monarcha Mundi* (Book III)." Evidently Weyer took the trouble to read the writings of this Italian as any contemporary psychiatrist would study the written productions of his patients. But "lest it appear strange to say, as I have, that the instruments of the imaginative virtue are thus affected and that the eyes of these poor little women (*mulierculae*) are dazzled, I would ask you to consider more closely the thoughts (that is, the ideational content — G. Z.) of these melancholics, their words, their visions and their actions (that is, their trends, attitudes and general behavior — G. Z.) and you will recognize to what extent their senses are depraved by the melancholic humor which is spread throughout their brains; and this presses so heavily on their minds that some of them think they are beasts, whose gestures and voices they even try to imitate; some think that they are earthenware, and therefore cautiously avoid meeting passers-by so as not to be broken by the encounter; others are afraid of death, and yet while suffering from this fear they frequently kill themselves; still others imagine that they are guilty of some crime and are so afraid that they tremble at the sight of anyone approaching, lest they be caught by the scruff of the neck, led to jail, and put to death by the Law. There was an old nobleman who would awake with a start thinking that he was being attacked by his enemies (so it seemed to him) taking him by force in order to shut him up in a furnace (Book III)." This description reads as a forecast of the excellent case histories of Philippe Pinel, and especially of Esquirol, which were to be written at the beginning of the nineteenth century and to be called *monomanias*.

Although there is no preponderance of women among the cases cited, it can be seen from Weyer's various references and remarks that women of every age were still, as in Sprenger's and Kraemer's time, the favorite target of the Inquisition. The misogyny of the *Malleus Maleficarum* has been discussed and emphasized in the first lecture. Weyer takes a definite stand in this respect and, contrary to tradition, holds the view that women should be punished less than men, and that they deserve more sympathy and understanding than man heretofore accorded them. In his own life and behavior, Weyer practised what he preached. He was married twice (his first wife died) and in both marriages his wife was not only his personal companion but his scientific and clinical collaborator. We recall, for example, Weyer's investigation of the fasting Barbara of Unn; as he was wont to do on such occasions, Weyer took the patient into his own house in order to study her with the help of his marital partner at close range. This more sympathetic attitude towards women may have developed in Weyer not quite accidentally; it is not impossible that in this respect the influence of his first master is a matter not to be neglected. Agrippa's loyalty and devotion to his wives (he was widowed twice) is well known — his loyalty appears even to have reached the point of a sentimental idealization of the female species. Weyer could not have overlooked Agrippa's treatise *On the Nobility and Pre-eminence of the Feminine Sex* which represents one of the most eloquent and fervent pieces of Agrippa's writing. Evidently such a treatise was one of the most expressive and safe ways to protest against witch-hunting and the abuses of the misogynous Inquisitors. Weyer concurred with Agrippa both in his views on the maltreatment of women and in his animated reaction to the most pressing of current social problems. The old dictum of St. Paul, *Femina sui corpore potestatem non habet sed vir* was thus argued as a point in favor rather than against women. However, the misogynous trend of the age was not to be bent by the views of Agrippa and Weyer. The ascetic monk, restrained in his instinctual life, was forced to project outward (in a manner so aptly described by Weyer himself) his own instinctual perceptions. The devil and particularly the *incubus* became the bearer of the monk's own projected instinctual impulses, and the witch or the *succubus* became the bearer of the monk's own source of instinctual perception. The ascete himself thus stood in the center of his psychotic projections and played the rôle of a relentless, cruel, and irreconcilable conscience. Paraphrasing St. Augustine, we may well say that in describing the attributes of God man tried to describe his own qualities, and in describing the attributes of Satan man described his own sinful propensities. With his definitions thus outlined, particularly in regard to the witch, man stood ready to hurl his cruelty against Satan and his every ally. Man, in his ascetic fervor and horror, could only ward off the pressure of his painful anxiety by assuming towards women the attitude so well defined by Pope Innocent III's remark to a Cardinal: "If one of us is to be confounded, I prefer that it should be you."

Weyer's open insistence that greater leniency be shown women, that even preferential treatment be accorded them, marks more than a simple humanistic trend. It indicates a profound change in the consciousness of man who, rising against the age-old ascetic tradition, stood ready to re-assume the responsibility for his own humanness. Instead of continuing to push his sense of sin into the overcrowded world of projections and paranoid delusions, man was now ready to shoulder the burden of it himself. Perhaps this re-alignment from projection to realistic self-perception was, more than any other factor, responsible for the individualization of man's mind. It naturally led to the emphasis of the value of the individual, increasing if not creating the humanism of the age, and augmenting the socialization of man's world view. Weyer was in the vanguard of this new psychological revolution, bringing the first inklings of a humanized, scientific, medical psychology into the midst of the prevailing confusion.

6

This process of individualization and humanization, probably the most important factor in the development of a sound medical psychology, was reflected in an interest in the *ideational content* of mental reactions rather than in their forms alone. *De praestigiis daemonum* is probably the only medical work with this advanced psychopathological viewpoint written before the pupils of Pinel began to make their contributions during the course of the first quarter of the nineteenth century (Esquirol, Georget, Falret, Bayle). It is perhaps the most complete, at any rate the most intelligent and scientific collection of psychopathological case histories that the sixteenth century has bequeathed to us. While it would be interesting to subject a good many of Weyer's cases to a detailed study — to reconstruct the various clinical characteristics of the age and thus to throw into relief certain nosological phenomena which undoubtedly are of great psychological and sociological value — such a study would take us too far afield and beyond the limited scope of this lecture. For since we are concerned here chiefly with placing Weyer in the proper historical light, our references to his understanding and management of individual cases will of necessity be limited.

Let us recall Weyer's scientific investigation of the case of the girl who was supposed to have vomited up wads of cloth. The methodical, rational, and systematic attitude displayed in this instance can be said to characterize Weyer's professional manner in the handling of all his cases. That Weyer, when discussing a case, frequently stresses the mistakes and foolishness of those who failed to differentiate mental disease from the maelstrom of general superstition is explained by the fact that *De praestigiis daemonum* is to a great extent a critical and even a polemical examination of certain actualities which were the very substance of the religious and social life of the day. Thus, for example, he tells of a peasant who was accused of wizardry, arrested, and convicted to death; the sentence would have been carried out were it not for the interference of his master who valued him highly as a worker; the convicted man was turned over to the custody of his lord who promised under oath to watch the poor wretch and guaranteed to protect the outside world against possible injuries the sick man might inflict on others. Returned to his home, the peasant was under the direct supervision of his master and began to eat good food. His health, both physical and mental, was restored within a comparatively short time (Book V). Weyer cites this case to demonstrate how erroneous and unjust the conviction of the peasant was, and how many a sick person would recover under proper treatment if his contemporaries were not so generous in dealing out death warrants.

Reflecting the limited horizon of the psychopathology of his day, Weyer cites another rather amusing story: " I want to tell you of a singular incident which is worthy of imitation. Philipp Nesselich of Cologne, a monk in the Abbey Kenechtsteden, was a simple and honorable man. In the year 1550 he began to be tormented by a spirit in the guise of a portly abbot who dragged him from one corner of the place to another — from the roof to the tower, over the walls, and about the garden. The spirit said that he was the departed Abbot Matthias of Düren, and that once he had commissioned a painter from Neuss to paint a beautiful picture of the Virgin, but that because he, Matthias, had failed to pay the man for his labor the poor painter had killed himself. The spirit asked Philipp to free him of his mental burden by going to Aachen and Trier and arranging that in each place three separate Masses be given for him. The theologians of Cologne advised that the wishes of the spirit be granted; all the monks of the monastery were of the same opinion and begged their abbot, Doctor Gerhard Strail-

gen von Noers, to concede the spirit's wishes. The
abbot, however, dissented; he admonished the sick
monk to cling to the living faith in the Mercy
of the Lord and to tell the spirit that he was under
the orders of his superiors and therefore not in a
position to make promises. The spirit, apprised
of this, replied to the monk: 'If this is the case,
then ask your sub-prior.' Whereupon the abbot
again admonished the monk, and noticing that the
latter had become very drowsy, threatened him, saying that if the monk would not listen to his orders he
would have him flogged in the presence of the whole
chapter. The abbot then once more advised the
monk to put his trust in God and immediately the
spirit disappeared to parts unknown and never to
return. I should advise (concludes Weyer) that this
method of treatment be generally applied to the
tricks of the devil (Book V)." Evidently Weyer
was more amused by, than concerned with, the hallucinatory loss of wits of the semi-stuporous monk;
this is the only instance, however, in his entire treatise when Weyer seems to approve of harshness and
threats of corporeal punishment in dealing with a
mentally sick person.[9]

[9] Weyer minces no words when he speaks of the execution of

In all other cases he remains consistently serene, composed, and kindly. Thus he tells us: "A Count whom I knew very well ordered two years ago that two women, suspected of witchraft, be tortured and burned. One of them was already dead as a result of torture when she was dragged out of the dungeon. As to the second, she confessed that with the help of a girl who had been in the employ of a noble lady, she used the various arts of witchcraft in order to make a certain nobleman lose his mind. This girl was also incarcerated and together with another man was most cruelly tortured and torn to pieces. I asked the Count to send me the written record of the statements made by both women, and accordingly one day the Count's trial judge arrived at my home. He told me the story and remarked that never before had he seen a more incredible capacity to withstand the severest torture. He said that in order to ascertain definitely that the woman was a witch the water test had been applied. The woman, tied in a knot as it were, was thrown into water to see whether she would sink or float. If she were innocent, she would drown, and if

the stuporous executioner of Antwerp, but in this case Weyer's wrath is self-understood.

171

she were a witch she would remain floating. I then demonstrated to the judge the error of his conclusion: I made it clear to him that the nobleman was not bewitched at all, but possessed by a demon.[10] This was the reason why they asked me to go and see that sick nobleman after a priest and a monk had tried in vain to chase the devil out of him. I then wrote the Count beseeching him, and I repeated my request through his judge, that he send the obviously innocent girl to me that I might care for her in my home; but the poor girl and the man were not freed from the henchmen until many months later. In the meantime, an evil spirit had intruded itself into the very family of the Count and the latter, at his most robust age, became a broken-down man who spent his days fettered to his bed (Book V}." This story is again illustrative of Weyer's steady and unrelenting scientific curiosity; he seldom speculates, he seldom argues, without gathering in advance all the pertinent facts in order to have a complete case history and to be able to reconstruct a clear-cut picture of the patient before his mind's eye. Although Weyer fails to give us sufficient detail to definitely establish the state-

---

[10] Here again Weyer uses this expression in its colloquial rather than in its purely literal sense.

ment, it is obvious that the Count was a sick man who suffered from some paranoid suspicions which he easily attached to some of his less noble subordinates — suspicions which led to the persecution of innocent people for alleged witchcraft. Evidently Weyer accurately sensed this situation and deliberately digressed from the history of the girl's case to the report that the Count himself had become mentally sick. This, despite Weyer's apparent reluctance to elaborate on the situation, testifies not only to his tactfulness, but also to his unusual intuition in matters of psychopathology.

Let us take, as an example of this, another case concerning a girl from the town of Burg who was thought to be possessed because, although a simple, uneducated girl who had always lived at home she spoke Latin.[11] "After a great deal of time was lost on conjurations," the girl finaly confessed that the spirit of Virgil had taken possession of her. Weyer pointed out that the girl's use of Latin words was quite a natural thing, because she was

[11] As we know, speaking an unknown language, particularly Latin or Greek, was in those days pathognomonic of being possessed by the devil; this symptom was one of the outstanding differential diagnostic points for the authors of the *Malleus* as well as for Ambroise Paré.

Tuscan and had always attempted to speak the Mantuan dialect — that is, the Lombardian language — which was closely related to Latin. Exorcisms having proven to be of no avail, a physician was called in who " cured her with the help of the Lord; he first used some medicaments which, as his art commanded him, purged the girl of black bile, and then he gave her some remedies ´ich had the virtue of making her physically stronger. Thus, the body having been purged, the Church could more easily deliver her from the evil spirit; for the physical obstacles having been removed, the priest could undertake the spiritual cure of the girl (Book V)."

While the humoral Galenic theory of mental diseases is constantly reflected in many of Weyer's recommendations, realization of the need to individualize the treatment of mentally sick people was by no means lacking. As a matter of fact, this individualization is as much a part of Weyer as is his humoral therapy. The following report characteristically demonstrates this point: " A certain woman named Bartholomea, who lived in the village of Well, had fallen into the habit of swooning during Mass, as if she were possessed by the devil, whenever the hymn *Gloria in excelsis Deo* was sung in

German instead of in Latin, and she remained in this state until the hymn was ended. She played this farce for a certain length of time without attracting attention. Finally Anna von Virmont, the Lady of the village, summoned Bartholomea to the palace and asked quietly and gently why it was that she let herself be overcome by the singing of that hymn, since the German words conformed exactly with the Latin text. Anna von Virmont then began to read the hymn in German, transposing it word for word from the Latin, and demonstrating as she went along that it contained nothing derogatory to the service of the Lord. She admonished the girl to be courageous, and then proceeded to sing the hymn in German, telling Bartholomea that if the sickness should overtake her she had an excellent remedy which had never failed to banish such devils. No sooner had she begun to sing than Bartholomea, choosing carefully the most comfortable spot, fell to the floor. Thereupon the honest and wise Lady called her chambermaid Katherina Biland, a woman of gentle spirit; together they lifted Bartholomea's skirts and switched her quite forcefully, though not transgressing the limits of reason. The possessed woman tried to pull down her skirts and began to defend herself as best she could. As Hippocrates has said, one should use severe remedies against severe and pernicious maladies. Anna von Virmont was thus able to persuade the patient that this medicine was a preservative of great virtue against such attacks of the devil. She said that learned men had taught her this method, and exhorted the girl to have more courage, assuring her that the greatest part of the devil's force was subdued by this procedure. Finally she resumed the singing of the hymn. This was all so well done that the sweet song was finished without Bartholomea's showing the least sign of disturbance. The servants of the house stood at the door of the room observing all this diligently, and as soon as Bartholomea left the room they grabbed her and went with her singing the same hymn in loud voices so that everybody could see that there was no more certain remedy to chase away the devil than the one used by Anna von Virmont. However, one should be very prudent in the use of such measures, because one cannot cure all eye maladies with the same eye-wash; this remedy acts promptly and is beneficial only if and when the person who is sick happens to will the sickness. This Bartholomea confessed to me personally that she was thus cured

176

in the Palace of Well through the remedy of the mistress of the palace (Book V)." Apparently there existed in those days a type of hysteria which represented a borderline condition between a more serious affliction and malingering.[12]

Weyer's attitude is clear; even when amused, even when approving of the use of the switch, he remains a systematic phychiatrist. First, he obtains a detailed story or written record; second, he talks to the patient personally whenever and wherever possible; third he follows up the case; fourth, he looks upon the whole procedure as a medical method which is true to the laws of physiology and psychology; and fifth, he looks upon the affliction as an illness *even when* he sees that in some cases the patient's will apparently participates in the production of the symptoms (malingering or similar behavior). In other words, Weyer discards the theological postulate of free will in so far as it remained the back-bone of the weird pseudo-psychiatry of the Inquisition and of traditional medicine. Weyer evidently believed that even abnormal behavior which had the appearance of being voluntary should be regarded as a psychopathological

[12] A somewhat similar mental condition is observed in our present-day " compensation cases."

problem — a contention which from the standpoint of scientific psychiatry is as advanced as it is pregnant with numerous potentialities. It is precisely this orientation in present-day psychiatry which made possible the most recent valuable contributions to the psychopathology of crime.[13] Once the pernicious stagnancy of the demonological tradition was overcome, Weyer seems to have uncovered all the horizons which were envisaged more clearly only by the centuries that succeeded him.

As for his immediate task, Weyer was naturally more preoccupied with dispelling the old than creating the new, and the business of unmasking the vanity of the various tricks which were used to alleviate the

[13] That this inference is not speculative but fully justified can be seen from the following lines taken from the twenty-third chapter of the Sixth Book: "If there is anyone (and in Weyer's day there were all too many—G. Z.) who contends that each wilful act must be punished yet more severely, I would ask him to bear in mind the distinction between the perfectly voluntary act of a sane person who behaves with a feeling that his mind is troubled and the act of a person whose will, if you permit me to say so, is so corrupted and out of control that the devil can play with it, giving the individual the appearance of being under some outside power. Such a disturbance (or defect) of one's will can also be imputed to melancholic individuals and little children. . . . The Lord who knows the kidneys and the heart does not permit that they be punished to the same extent as those whose minds are free (sane); so much less right has man to mete out punishment on such people."

178

mentally sick claimed his first attention. We know
how opposed he was to the crass charlatanery around
him and how skilfully he exposed it, but it was difficult to disabuse the honest believers in the magic
qualities of things which would have been innocuous
if they had not bred and upheld superstition. Weyer
viewed these honest believers as " blind in both eyes
— both mental and physical." We cite here an example to illustrate how Weyer tried to enlighten not
only the magic faith-healers, but the patients themselves whose insight into their own troubles he considered even at that time the most potent therapeutic
factor. "A young girl who was tormented by an evil
spirit was given by a priest a piece of paper wrapped
in leather to wear around her neck as a remedy. This,
he said, would help her but she must be careful not
to lose it or her trouble would return. The girl was
very careful and took great pains not to lose the
charm. Judith, my wife, heard about the affair and
asked the girl to come to see her. She admonished
the girl to place her trust only in the Lord, the Pro-
tector of all sufferers, and to scorn the devil's doings.
Then she gave her to eat and to drink, and took the
piece of paper wrapped in leather which was hanging from the girl's neck. Those present were fright-

179

ened and they all ran away because they were afraid
that the girl would again enter one of her states of
horrible excitement. The girl was thus left alone
with my wife and my daughter Sophie; nothing happened to the sick girl. My wife opened the leather
container and found inside a piece of paper that was
folded over many times; nothing was found to be
written on it. In the presence of the patient she
threw the piece of paper into the fire. The patient,
calmed by the admonition of my wife, developed a
good appetite and appeared quite cheerful and con-
tented . . . and in so far as I know she remained
well from that time forward (Book V)." *Sapienti sat.*

7

From the cases and examples cited above, it can
be seen that Weyer's considerations and analyses of
demoniacal possessions and witchcraft have covered
the majority if not all of the clinical psychopathological conditions met with in the sixteenth century
with one exception — the mass-neuroses or the mass-
psychoses which were characteristic of and prevalent
throughout the Middle Ages, the Renaissance, the
seventeenth century, and which were occasionally met
with in the eighteenth and even in the nineteenth cen-

turies. According to De Moray, for instance, the last such outbreak took place in France in 1878. These mass-psychopathies which always appeared to be in the nature of epidemics, Weyer treats in his usual studious but practical manner.

The epidemics were most frequently met with in monasteries and convents; they presented quite naturally many complex problems and were the cause of endless theological hair-splitting. As usual, Weyer stands apart from the theological and other purely theoretical controversies, and keeps in touch with various institutions, such as orphanages, convents, and monasteries, in order to find out what specific types of mental disturbances were prevalent among congregations of individuals living uniform and seemingly well-regulated lives together. He devotes several chapters of the Fourth Book of his treatise to this question, telling of some mental disturbances among young children (chapter eight) and referring in particular to an epidemic of mental disease which had broken out in a Roman orphanage hospital in 1555 and had continued almost two years, affecting about seventy young girls. Chapter ten is concerned with " The Nuns of Uvertet who were demoniacal and who were thought to have been

bewitched by the witches;" chapter eleven is entitled "The diabolic torments which occurred in
the Monastery of Kentorp and which were imputed
to witches;" and the story related in chapter twelve,
"The history of the Nuns of the Convent of Nazareth at Cologne who were afflicted by the devil," we
cite here in some detail.

For some years these nuns had been intermittently
disturbed by the devil; the trouble climaxed in 1564.
Weyer organized an investigation on the twenty-fifth
of May, 1565 "in the presence of the following noble
and wise persons: Constantin of Lyskerken, Coun-
sellor; Master Johann Altenan, formerly Dean of
Cleve; Master Johann Echt, Doctor of Medicine; and
my son Heinrich, Doctor of Philosophy and Medicine." The nuns were subject to frequent attacks of
peculiar convulsions during which they closed their
eyes and lay on their backs with their abdomens ele-
vated. Weyer recognizes the obvious erotic nature of
the convulsions, observing that the nuns, when
the attack was over, "would open their eyes with an
apparent expression of shame and would look as if
they had endured a great deal of pain." "A girl named
Gertrude, who was fourteen years old and lived in
this convent gave the first cause for all this mis-

fortune. She often suffered from insane apparitions while in bed . . ." and was first discovered by the noises she made when trying to chase away her imaginary lover. " One of her companions came to sleep on a cot near the room of Gertrude expressly to defend her against the apparition, but the poor thing became very frightened as soon as she began to hear the usual noise." As a result this nun, too, succumbed to a breakdown. " During the attack it appeared as if she was unable to see well, while at other times she appeared quite normal, although she used very strange words. . . . Soon others joined her in her peculiar behavior . . . the poor afflicted nuns became much worse when they began to resort to irregular remedies." Weyer also observes that whenever an epidemic of the pest (typhoid fever?) broke out the mental condition of the nuns would clear up, but that no sooner had they recovered from the fever than the convulsive states and the mental confusion would return. The investigation made by Weyer and his " Committee " disclosed the following rather realistic pathogensis: The affair started when a few young men of the neighborhood, probably drunk, became acquainted with " one or two of the nuns and following this they repeated their visits

183

by negotiating the wall and enjoying a love affair with them." After this was stopped, "the devil spoiled the fantasy of these miserable girls and offered them in their imagination" what they missed in reality. Weyer kept in touch with the nuns, particularly with those who were the original source of the trouble, and "explained to them amply in letters which I sent to them, what decent and Christian means to use in order to forget the tragedy."

Weyer returns to the problem in Book VI: "If one finds several bewitched or demoniacal persons at one and the same place, as ordinarily happens in monasteries and convents, particularly in the latter, because women are the most convenient butt for the evil pranks of Satan, it is necessary before all things to separate them from each other and to see to it that they be sent back to their respective parents or relatives, in whose homes they could more conveniently be cured; however, this should be done *always taking into consideration the individual needs of each person; one should avoid, as the expression goes, moulding them all in accordance with one definite model*,[14] as is the custom of many inept people, liars, impostors, and various other grand

---

[14] The italics are ours.

masters of superstition and impiety." Weyer then goes on to say that while there are nuns who are not permitted to leave the enclosure of the convent ("which practice I certainly am unable to approve") and others who might prefer to do penance and endure their illness as best they can, it is very important that "the young nuns should be spared from seeing such spectacles" because they are very susceptible to such things and they might catch the same illness. Weyer relates further a number of reports obtained by direct correspondence with various nuns, telling of octogenerian, chronically psychotic women who had pined their lives away for years in their respective nunneries, of young girls who had suffered from severe attacks of major hysteria over a long period of time, and of various mass-psychopathies. Evidently Weyer was a prodigious letter writer, and through this medium was able to keep in close touch with the psychopathology of various monasteries and convents. On another occasion Weyer speaks of Judith, a young novice at the Convent of Bosleduc near the Cathedral of Saint John the Baptist. "I saw (her) tormented by the devil with strange convulsions. Her throat was so contracted that she was unable to swallow

185

any meat (*globus hystericus?* — G. Z.) and her tongue was held in such a manner that she was unable to speak; [15] and yet on other occasions I heard her say most ridiculous and horrible things." Thus Weyer continues in his own practice what he advises others to do — that is, he individualizes the psychopathological problems with which he has to deal.

8

This broad outline of Johann Weyer — of his life, his personality, and his *De praestigiis daemonum* — practically concludes our review of Weyer's formal contribution to the psychopathology of the sixteenth century and particularly to psychopathology in general. Were we to bring this series of lectures to a close at this point, however, several unanswered questions would naturally arise: What was Weyer's influence on his public and, more specifically, on his colleagues? What were the immediate repercussions of *De praestigiis daemonum* and its ultimate fate? And finally, what historical position does Weyer

[15] The original text is couched in a somewhat more colloquial language: " He (the devil) pressed her throat so hard . . . and he (the devil) kept her tongue in such a strange manner. . . ." However, as has been repeatedly pointed out, Weyer's conception of the devil was not the traditional superstitious one.

occupy in the field of psychiatry? While these questions cannot be answered in detail within the limited framework of this series, it is obvious that they deserve at least some consideration, for a mere factual report about a great physician of the sixteenth century does not reconstruct the historical perspective of his endeavors, nor does it make it possible for us, as medical men, to visualize those elements of pragmatic continuity of thought without which history is not history.

That Weyer should have exercised an immediate and telling influence on his public is too much to expect; no matter what the age or the generation, radical innovators are seldom recognized as sound leaders by their contemporaries. Moreover, Weyer was dealing with a problem loaded with enormous and explosive charges of emotion. To borrow an apt phrase from Binz, "Weyer was talking like a rational human being to the inmates of a gigantic insane asylum and undoubtedly with the same success." There were a few thoughtful men, however, who responded to the publication of *De praestigiis daemonum* with enthusiasm. As many as three physicians sent congratulatory letters; the Jurist Caspar Borcholt addressed the Council of Braunschweig calling sympathetic attention to Weyer's views; Bishop Simon Sulzer of Basel gave him high praise, and instigated the German translation of the treatise three years after its appearance in Latin; a Benedictine abbot, Anton Hovaeus of Echternach, although deeming it both necessary and wise to conceal his name, wrote a letter signed with his initials: " I know of no book that I have read, nay swallowed, with greater good and deeper spiritual joy, than I have yours. It is my opinion that this book will bring your name into the future adorned with immortal glory "; [16] and still another ecclesiastic, a preacher, addressed him: " . . . In a word, Domine Weyer, the divine salve of thy book with which thou hast opened the many eyes darkened with impurity, pleases me. People will easily see that it is a gift from on High and it will be received with open arms, nay, he who will read it with common sense and understanding, will also be less afraid of the magic arts." With these few enthusiastic followers, the list of Weyer's new and influential adherents acquired through the publication of *De praestigiis daemonum*, while not fully exhausted, is more or less complete.

[16] Binz, Carl, *op. cit.*, p. 66.

The second half of the sixteenth century was a turbulent and bloody period, the real spirit of which was more truthfully reflected by Judge Boguet [17] than by a profound medical thinker. Weyer, finishing his treatise with the sad realization of the futility of measuring his efforts with an overwhelming opposition, made a last serious attempt to convince his contemporaries that he did not harbor any destructive ideas, implored his readers to listen to reason, and admonished, even challenged them, to state their objections to his work openly and fully. But " It appears that all this was of comparatively little use; at a meeting of the Princes of the Rhineland held near Bingen soon after the appearance of the first edition, Weyer's book was discussed and the Pfälz Chancellor, Dr. Christof Probus, spoke about it in a most warm and laudatory manner ... (but) the pyromania of the Theological Faculty of Heidelberg was only partially diminished, and as for Mainz, Trier, and Cologne, those were words thrown to the wind." [18] Weyer himself was not psychologically unprepared: " I have no doubt," he says, " that many people will view my work with anger and irritation. They will reproach me for what they will

[17] Cf. Lecture Two.   [18] Binz, Carl, *op. cit.*, p. 64.

fail to understand. . . . Others will try not to miss an opportunity to sink their malicious teeth into me; most of the theologians will write and say that it is not seemly for a physician to step out beyond the confines of his profession. . . . If they complain that I attacked them unjustly, I do not object to their coming out into the open and publicly defending their cause against me." Again: " If any arguments prove unsatisfactory to some learned and sensitive members of our profession — to which, knowing my humble capacity, I freely accede — I feel that at least to the best of my ability, I offer them the opportunity to weigh and examine the matter with greater precision, to employ a more scientific method and a more systematic order, a trend of thought more clear, words more suitable and arguments more true, more forceful and more convincing. If I am admonished for and convinced of having committed an error I shall be grateful to those who will point it out to me; I shall never be ashamed to retract my mistakes, for I am not so good a friend of my own self that I would refuse to recognize my mistakes."

After appealing to the reader to consider calmly and reasonably what is fair and just, Weyer names those wise and human Princes of his day who follow the advice of their hearts and who struggle against superstition. Quite naturally the name of his own Prince, Duke Wilhelm Cleve, occupies the first place among those who were the most progressive in the matter of dealing with the alleged witches. He then adds: " Although I answered fully to this (various arguments in favor of the traditional belief in witchcraft) in the Third Book, chapters three and four, I should like to add a few more words, and first of all ask, how do you know that they (the witches) have made a pact with the devil? You will agree with me that you were not present at the conclusion of this pact and that you never heard anyone worth believing who had witnessed it himself. This knowledge, then, is acquired solely through the confession of these poor old stupid and troubled women, and the confession is either voluntary or given under stress. If it is the latter, then it is imperfect and of no value, because it was exacted under the unbearable pains of torture; is there anything more dangerous than to depend, in such complicated matters, with no eye-witnesses to be found, solely on the confession of an old woman who has lost her mind? I am sure that you would not persist in your opinion if you had personally seen how boiling oil is poured on their legs, how they are burned under the armpits with lighted candles, and how these poor old innocent women are subjected to an infinite number of other cruel and barbaric torments."

Weyer's final words are a reminder of Horace's mockery of the magic horrors, nocturnal spirits, and iniquitous witches which were supposed to have filled ancient Thessaly. Then he says: " I do not pretend to have stated anything in this book that I am not ready to submit in whole or in part to the most equitable judgment of the Catholic Church of Our Lord Jesus Christ, and I stand ready to correct and to retract anything that will be convincingly shown to me to be an error." This pious conclusion is not merely a rhetorical bow, as one might suppose, nor is it a concession to the spirit of the time.

Weyer was a genuinely religious man who sincerely and rightly saw no conflict between his liberal views and the Church. In spite of this the authorities placed him, as *auctor primae classis*, on the *Index librorum prohibitorum*, which meant that not only *De praestigiis daemonum*, but all his other writings, were forbidden. The fact that Weyer's name appears on a number of local *Indices librorum prohibitorum* in Germany, France, Italy, and Spain proves that the book became quickly known all over Europe. There is also more direct evidence of the increasing popularity of Weyer's writings among the silent readers of the time. Within one year after the appearance of *De praestigiis* a second edition was issued (1564), augmented by almost ninety pages and containing, among others, the congratulatory letter of the Benedictine abbot Hovaeus. Weyer reproduced only the initials of the latter because " I prefer to pass over in silence the name of the distinguished theologian who is known for his learning, charity, and respect in which people hold him; I do so in order not to arouse the anger of some who happen to adorn themselves with the names, titles, and caps of theologians." Three years later (1566) a third edition appeared covering 745 pages instead of the 479 of the original edition. One year later Weyer's own translation into the vernacular was published. A new edition was issued in 1568 to which Book VI was added, and other new editions of *De praestigiis* followed in 1577 and 1583, five years before Weyer's death. The *Opera omnia* appeared in 1660. In other words, even during Weyer's lifetime the treatise gained in popularity and author-

ity and quite naturally opposition to it arose in corres-
ponding proportion.[19] The specific reason for this
strong opposition is well defined by Carl Binz: "As
far as one can humanly judge, there is reason to assume that the success of Weyer's book would have
been greater and more lasting if he had stressed only
the argument which really required no further proof—
namely, that torture, by its very nature, was capable
of exacting any sort of 'confession' one could imagine. But Weyer's thesis was that witches were
women whom the devil had made melancholic and
insane, and that as a result of their abnormal mental
state they would always confess to having accom-
plished things which they had never really done nor
been able to do. This is Weyer's incessant and ever
recurrent refrain, beginning with the title of the book
and lasting until its closing lines." [20] In other words,
what irked his contemporaries was exactly that part
of Weyer's thought which formed his chief scientific
contribution to psychological medicine. This point

[19] In 1581 the Portuguese Inquisition put Weyer on the *Index*
as *Auctor secundae classis*, thus limiting the prohibition only to
De praestigiis daemonum. The Spanish Inquisition did likewise in
1583, but in 1590 and 1596 the revised *Index* which was begun
in Trent and completed in Rome reestablished Weyer as *Auctor
primae classis*, which place he still occupies.

[20] Binz, Carl, *op. cit.*, p. 69.

cannot be overlooked if we are to evaluate properly Weyer's historical rôle as well as the historical dynamics of the relationships between medicine and psychiatry. The persistence in the belief that witches did exist, that their existence could not be questioned, that their hallucinatory or delusionary statements were truths, betrays a singular psychology that cannot be lightly dismissed. The belief became a postulate, a dogma as it were, which was definitely not to be probed or investigated by any scientific mind. We have shown how the witch, the devil, and their inseparable companionship fulfilled an *emotional* and not an *intellectual* need of the age; hence to admit that her very existence was a delusion meant abandoning the entire artificial scaffolding of one's distorted instinctual life and surrendering one's self to one's own elemental subjective affects. Such a psychological state, whatever its external aspects, was dictated by an internal despair; it was this inner state that had to keep the witch alive in order to kill her. Michelet's remark that " the witch was born out of the despair of humanity," though intuitive, could not have been more exactly right; it was the same sort of intuition, perhaps, which inspired Weyer to dub Satan as *Milleartifex*. To what extent this desperate need for the witch was dominating the minds of men, we may judge from the nature of the opposition that was raised against Weyer by some of the most learned men of his generation.

Foremost among them was Jean Bodin (1530-1596) whose reputation of liberal philosopher, preacher of tolerance, and learned jurist reached far and wide, persisting even to our day. One could hardly accuse such a man of having been a fervent adherent to the Roman Catholic dogma *per se,* or of having lacked stamina or intellect. Nothing but severe affects could have so aroused his rage against Weyer, "the little doctor" who dared to contest what was asserted by "the Laws of the Twelve Tables, great Jurists and Emperors, the Inquisitors, and great people such as the Persians, the Hebrews, the Greeks, the Romans, the French, Italians, Spaniards, and the English." [21] It was Bodin's reformistic bent that won him a place on the *Index librorum prohibitorum,* and *not* his opposition to Weyer. He rebelled, to use his own words, against " the apostasy of urine," that is, against the presumptions of a medical man who dared to approach the problem of

[21] Bodin against Weyer in his *Traité de la démonomanie des sorciers,* published in 1579.

196

witchcraft with a scientific detachment. To Weyer's discussion of lycanthropy and delusions of being an animal, Bodin had but one answer, an exclamation of venom and disgust: And how about Nebuchad-nezzar who became a bull and ate grass?! Bodin's treatise, published almost one hundred years after the appearance of the *Malleus*, differs in no respect from the latter. As a jurist, Bodin had not advanced a single step beyond Sprenger and Kraemer. He re-lates, at the opening of his treatise, the case of a woman from Compiègne who allegedly had had rela-tions with the devil since her twelfth year and had continued them after marriage. Several of the judges, " by nature somewhat more mild and sympa-thetic " than the others, wished to have her hanged, but Bodin fought against them and managed that the psychotic woman be burned alive. Bodin thought that Weyer himself was a wizard and an ally of the witches, and that because he pleaded the cause of the witches so persistently he was " singing in the dark " to hide his fear of the fate which might be meted out to him as a result of this intimacy with the nefarious.

Delrio, a learned Jesuit (1551-1608) to whom Weyer was *Wierus hereticus,* found no kinder words for Weyer than did Jean Bodin. Delrio speaks of

Wieri deliria and gives vent to his indignation: "Why? If doctors were permitted to express their opinions, no one would be burned!"[22] In spite of his learning, Delrio was but a sixteenth century Jesuit copy of the fifteenth century Dominican, and true to the pattern was not loath to use unfair arguments against Weyer. He quotes Bartholomeus de Spina as saying: "Satan in the guise of a Prince once addressed a gathering of wizards and witches. 'Console yourselves,' he said, 'in another few years you will triumph over all good Christians, for the efforts of Weyer and his followers lend me considerable support in my opposition to the Father-Inquisitor.' He then stated to them that were it not for people like Weyer, his (Satan's) subordinates, the wizards and witches, would have been conquered by the Inquisitors or at least they would have been exiled from all Christian countries." The dubious cast of this quotation becomes clear when we learn that Bartholomeus de Spina died in 1546, that is, before Weyer wrote his book and before Delrio was born.[23]

[22] Delrio, M. A., *Disquisitionum magicarum* (Mainz, 1593), Book VI, Section 16.

[23] J. Buchmaan, studying and comparing original texts, states that the above quotation from De Spina refers directly and by name to the Jurist Ponzinibius, a liberal thinker of Northern Italy. Cf. Binz, Carl, *op. cit.*

Sixtus of Siena called Weyer *valde insanus,* and the protestant voice of Johannes Brentz joined in the chorus of indignation.

Weyer found less cruelty but no more understanding among his medical colleagues, some of whom, like Hermann Neuwald, Professor of Medicine in Helmstaedt, or Andreas Masius, were close personal friends. The latter read the manuscript of the book and wrote to Weyer: " It is a raw piece of work, put together without sense or understanding. . . . You ought to rewrite it in part, and in part destroy it." Thomas Graftus, Professor of Medicine in Heidelberg, was even more definite and more vehement. Scribonius, the well-known physician from Marburg and Korbach, rose against Weyer's psychopathology, rejecting as nonsensical the entire treatise, and even opposing Weyer's criticism of the water test: " This Weyer, in order to engage the judges in favor of the witches, tries to prove that their behavior is a result of unhealthy imagination and of fantasies created by various sleeping potions; in other words (Weyer tries to prove) that witches only imagine their crimes, but that in reality they have done nothing untoward! Weyer does nothing more than remove the guilt from the shoulders of the witches to free

them from the need of any punishment; all this —
only in order to bring into vogue all the art and all
the friends of witchcraft! Yes, I shall say it openly:
with Bodin, I believe that Weyer has consecrated
himself to the witches, that he is their comrade and
companion in crime, that he himself is a wizard and
a mixer of poisons who has taken upon himself the
defense of other wizards and poison-mixers. Oh, if
only such a man had never been born, or at least had
not written anything! Instead of which, he gives
many people through his books the opportunity to
sin and to enhance the Kingdom of Satan." [24] Scribonius thus expresses ironically enough the unspoken
thoughts of the medical profession as, with superfi-
cial deference, it follows the cortège funèbre.
"Weyer died tired of the spirit of his age" on the
twenty-fourth of February, 1588, in Tecklenburg;
he was buried in the church-yard of the local church,
but no trace of the church nor of the tomb is now
extant.[25]

[24] Quoted by Binz from *G. A. Scribonius, De sagarum natura et
potestate, deque his recte cognoscendis et putriendis physiologia*
(Marburg, 1588).

[25] Shortly before his death Weyer sustained a severe psychological blow; his favorite Duke Wilhelm of Jülich-Cleve-Berg, who
had suffered a stroke some time previously, developed a psychosis,

If spiritual isolation followed Weyer to his grave, his influence was restored in the succeeding century. The process was slow, often painful, and in some of its more delicate refinements has yet to be completed, but it suffices to mention such names as Friedrich of Spee and Cornelius Loos to recall that what was known at first as " Weyer's poison " gradually percolated and found its victorious expression. Everyone, regardless of business or professional standing, continued to fight a medical man when he attempted to establish a sound medical psychology. There is no better illustration of this attitude than the reference to Weyer in the revised Saxon criminal code — the *Consultationes Saxonicae* of 1572. According to this code a witch, even if she had caused no harm, was to be put to death; direct reference is then made to Weyer's views and it is stated: " Weyer's mode of thinking is of no great importance, since he was a medical man and not a jurist." [26] The jurist, lay and

and so did the son; a riot of witch-hunting ensued, forcing Weyer to flee to Tecklenburg. Cf. Kirchhoff, Theodor, *Deutsche Irren-ärtzte*, 2 vols. (Berlin, 1921), Vol. I, p. 5.

[26] " Es sind längst verschienene Jahre viel Bücher ausgangen, darinnen die Zauberei mehr vor ein Superstition und Melancholey dann vor ein Ubelthat gehalten, und wird hart darauf gedrungen, dass dieselbe am Leben nicht zu strafen. *Des Wieri rationes seyn*

ecclesiastic, remained at the helm. Delrio's *Disquisitionum magicarum* went through fourteen editions before 1736 and his book appeared in England in 1606, where it was published at the expense of King James I, himself the author of a book entitled *Demonologie*. The latter was supposed to be a refutation of Reginald Scot's *The Discoverie of Witchcraft*, written under the influence of Weyer and destroyed by order of King James. The jurist was in fact all-powerful: the last witch to be killed in Germany was Anna Maria Schwägelin, decapitated in Menningen, Bavaria, on March 30, 1775; in Glarus, Switzerland, a servant girl was decapitated on June 18, 1782, exactly two hundred and twenty years after *De praestigiis daemonum* was written. One should not overlook, however, that isolated acts of enlightened awakening could be uncovered here and there — ten years after Weyer's death De Thou, President of the Parliament of Paris, led his assembly in 1598 to revoke an order issued for the arrest and death of a psychotic in Angers; the sick man was ordered, instead, to be committed temporarily to a hospital.

nicht sehr wichtig, als der ein Medicus und nicht ein Jurist gewesen. So ists ein geringes Fundament, dass er meynet, die Weiber werden nicht leiblich zum Tanz und Teufelsgespenste geführt, . . ."

Anne Hendriks burnt in Amsterdam A° 1571

9

Weyer evinced enthusiasm and pride in his medical calling in every possible way. Two of his sons were physicians; one — Heinrich — he mentioned in his report on the psychopathic epidemic which broke out among the Augustinian nuns in the Convent of Nazareth near Cologne; the other — Galenus — Weyer baptized with a name characteristic of his own medical ideas. This constant reference to his medical calling, repeated often enough by Weyer himself and not less emphatically reiterated in this lecture, is more than a manner of speaking or an unusual pride in one's profession. It reflects a fact that is replete with historical meaning. Weyer insisted that medical knowledge was a prerequisite for treating with witches, and the world opposed him in this view. At face value this situation appears anomalous. It is of great significance for the historian of medicine since in the development of medical science exactly the reverse position is the rule: Man is sick, he knows he is sick, and therefore he seeks help from one who happens to know what to do with and for a sick person. The doctor is the product of man's needs, and as these needs have increased, the doctor's knowledge and skill have grown in proportion. Medicine, then, has actually been born out of the pressure of circumstance. This natural development has been completely reversed in the evolution of medical psychology. Hippocrates had to convince his contemporaries that the sacred disease was not sacred at all, and that it could and should be treated by a doctor. Weyer had to convince his contemporaries that the cursed state of witchcraft or of being bewitched was not cursed and was not a crime but a disease which a doctor could and should treat. This perhaps is the reason why psychiatry entered the fold of medicine later than any other branch of medical knowledge and why it trailed behind the other medical specialities. It is not without interest in this connection to point out that while a great many non-medical men made substantial contributions to many branches of medicine, psychology — that is, academic psychology — contributed little if anything to psychopathology. The process is here also reversed in that medical psychology has always been the pioneer in the general field, stimulating the most important advances in the study of normal psychology. Therein lies the greatest historical significance of Johann Weyer, for he was the first medical man to insist that normal and pathological mental processes differ in degree and form but not in substance, and that human will has nothing to do with mental sickness.

It is this point of view, courageously stated and valiantly defended, that gives Weyer the right to be called the founder of modern psychiatry. Weyer's historical contribution is not his humane attitude towards witches, nor even his emphatic recognition that witches were mentally sick women, but his founding of a real clinical psychopathology which endured in spite of every cruel opposition. The seventeenth and eighteenth centuries imperceptibly, at times unknowingly, followed the clinical path first broken by Weyer. In short, Weyer's accomplishment was two-fold: first, he introduced the scientific, descriptive, observational method to clinical psychopathology, and second, he reclaimed the whole field of psychopathology for medicine. Needless to say, the success of this task was neither rapid nor immediately obvious; one may properly recall the words of Francis Bacon: "Medicine is a science which hath been, as we have said, more professed than labored, and yet more labored than advanced;

the labor having been in my judgment, rather in a circle than in progression." [27]

The sixteenth century came to a close with a definite attempt and even a determined effort to study man's behavior in a systematic, scientific way. This new principle is best summarized in the same treatise by Francis Bacon: "The first article on the culture of mind will regard the different natures or dispositions of men . . . so that an artificial [28] and accurate dissection may be made of men's minds and nature and the secret disposition of each man laid open that from a knowledge of the whole, the precepts concerning the cures [29] of the mind may be more rightly formed. And not only the characters of dispositions impressed by nature should be received into this treatise, but those also which are otherwise imposed upon the mind by the sex, age, country, state of health, make of body, etc. And again, those which proceed from fortune as princes, nobles, common people, the rich, the poor, the magistrates, the ignorant, the happy, the miserable." Here we have a

[27] Bacon, Francis, *Proficience and Advancement of Learning,* Book Two.

[28] This word meant "scientific" in the sixteenth and seventeenth centuries.

[29] That is, culture.

brief outline of what has been done on the ground-work together with a plan for future work which the sixteenth century has bequeathed to the future psychiatrist. And in this bequest Weyer's was a major contribution of leadership and performance.

Çomment · l'églife · eſt · reprefentée · et · les · ſtʒiracles · quy ſy · font · par · l'intʒsſiun · du · ſ͂ · oú · les · pélerius · ſe randent · en · grande · ðevation ·

Exorcism of the mentally sick in the
Church of Bonnet

(A drawing by Abbot Frusotte after one of nine-teen frescoes of the XV century)

207

INDEX

A

Adrian VI (Pope), 23
Agrippa, Cornelius, 70, 103-08, 112-13, 134-36, 164
Agrippa's dog, 104, 134-36
albealion, see nightmare
alcranum, see nightmare
amulets, 46, 179-80
anesthesia, hysterical, 49
anthropologia, 103
Antipalus Maleficarum, 24
Antony, Saint, 52
Aquinas, Thomas, 15
Aristotle, 31, 51, 52, 53
arsenic, 143
asceticism, 56, 61, 165
atrabile, *see* bile, black
atresias, 124
atropin, 144
Augustine, Saint, 3, 12, 32-33, 45-46, 76, 165
Averroes, 156
Avicenna, 31, 156

B

babies, slaying of, 18, 57-58, 137, 142
Bacon, Francis, 71, 205, 206
Bacon, Roger, 15
Barbara of Unn, case of, 125-26, 164
Bartholomea, case of, 174-77
Bayle, Antoine, 167
belladona, 144, 146
Benedict, Saint, 61
Bénet, Armand, 65

bile, black, 90, 152, 158, 174
Binz, Carl, 4, 23, 187, 188, 189, 194
Bloomingdale Hospital, ix, 18
bodies, foreign, *see* foreign bodies
Bodin, Jean, 3, 82, 196-97
Boguet, 73-75, 189
Borcholt, Caspar, 187
Brahe, Tycho, 70
Brandeburg, Joachim of, 24
Braunschweig, Council of, 187
Brentz, Johannes, 199
Brett, George Sidney, 25, 76
Buchmaan, J., 198
Bulls, *see* Gregory IX (Pope), Bull of; Innocent VIII (Pope), Bull of
Butler, Samuel, 135

C

Calmeil, L.-F., 73
cannabis indica, 144
cantharides, 143
Cardanus, 70
Celsus, 3
charms, 46, 179-80
children, *see* babies, slaying of
chronicity (in witchcraft), 47, 140
Cibo, Giovanni Battista, 23
Codex Theodosianus, 13
compulsion neuroses, 63
confessions, *see* witches, confessions of
conscience, 97-98, 165